WINDOWS 11 FOR SENIORS MADE EASY

Who Needs Tech Support?

By James Bernstein

Bernstein, James
Windows 11 for Seniors Made Easy
Part of the Computers For Seniors Made Easy series

For more information on reproducing sections of this book or sales of
this book, go to **www.madeeasybookseries.com**

Contents

Introduction

These days everyone has a desktop computer, laptop, or at least a device such as a smartphone or a tablet that they use to do things such as go online, send emails, and so on. And for the people who use a personal computer at home or at work, then there is a very good chance that it is running Microsoft Windows and if it's not, then you are most likely using a Mac and are reading the wrong book!

When Windows 10 first came out, Microsoft has said that it would be the last version of their desktop operating system and that they would just continue to update it and add new features rather than come out with new versions. But now that Windows 11 is out, that proves what many of us always believed, that there would eventually be a replacement for Windows 10. And when a company releases new software, they feel the need to change things around to make it look like it has been "upgraded" but many times, they are making changes just to justify calling it new!

The goal of this book is to help you get the most out of your Windows 11 computer and make you a more proficient computer user. I will cover the basics (in detail) to better help you understand how to do things like open programs, locate your files, customize your desktop, install apps and games, browse the internet, navigate the Windows Start menu and more.

I always like to take a step-by-step approach so users at any skill level will be able to follow along. I will also include many screenshots to help you see what I am discussing in case you want to follow along on your own computer. One thing to keep in mind is that since Microsoft is constantly updating Windows that if you come across something in this book that doesn't match up with what your computer shows, it's most likely that Microsoft has changed how you do that procedure!

So, on that note, let's get things started and turn you into a Windows 11 expert, or at least get you a few steps closer!

Chapter 1 – Getting Started

If you are totally new to using computers, then it's easy to see how you can be intimidated by them or not even want to try and learn how to use one. But just like with anything else in life, once you figure it out and get comfortable with it, you wonder how you were ever afraid to try in the first place.

Now let's say you just got yourself a new computer and this one has the latest and greatest version of Windows while your previous computer had an older version, and things look quite a bit different. This can be intimidating as well but fortunately, it's just a case of learning how to do the same things a bit differently or even just a case of things working exactly the same, but the icons and colors have changed.

Whatever the case may be, after reading this book you should have a much better handle on how to use your new or existing computer and might actually start enjoying it!

Using Windows 11 for the First Time
If you are upgrading from Windows 10 or have bought a new computer that came with Windows 11, there are a few things you will need to get used to. For the most part, the learning curve is not too steep if you are the type of user who just does the basics such type documents, surf the internet and check email.

If you are a Windows power user, then that is a different story since there are a lot of things that have changed from the older Windows 10 operating system. But since this book is about Windows 11 basics, we don't need to worry about that kind of stuff.

If you find that you want to learn about more of the advanced features of Windows 11, then check out my book titled **Windows 11 Made Easy.**
https://www.amazon.com/dp/B09HFXWXRY

The main visual difference between Windows 11 and Windows 10 that you will notice is the Start Menu looks and operates and the Start button and pinned icons are placed in the center of the taskbar rather than on the left side of it. The Start Button is the icon with the four boxes which is meant to represent a window (for Windows).

Figure 1.1 shows the Windows 10 Start Button and search box while figure 1.2 shows the Windows 11 Start button, search icon and other pinned apps. I will be discussing the Start menu in more detail in chapter 2.

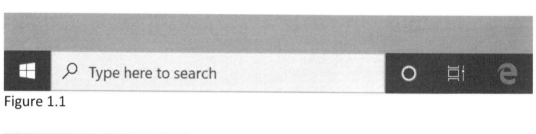

Figure 1.1

Figure 1.2

When you click on the Start button to view the Start Menu, you will also notice how things have changed there as well. Figure 1.3 shows the Windows 10 Start Menu while figure 1.4 shows the Windows 11 Start Menu.

Figure 1.3

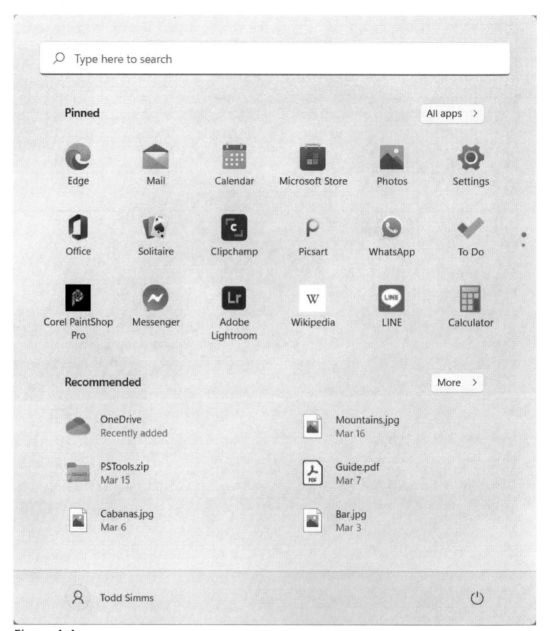

Figure 1.4

Once you get used to the new Start Menu and taskbar, you should be ok since the other changes are more appearance related such as the way the icons look and the overall Windows color scheme.

Microsoft Account

If you have been using Windows for some time, you might be used to having a username and password to log into your computer. Over the past several years, Microsoft has pushed its customers to use what they call a Microsoft account to login to your computer with.

A Microsoft account is basically an email address that you use for Microsoft related services so that you only need to remember one login for everything you do. It is free to sign up for a Microsoft account and there is a good chance you already have one. If not, you will need to create one to log into your computer with.

When you turn on your computer for the first time, you will be taken through a setup process to configure your preferences and create your Windows user account. If you don't have a Microsoft account, then you will be able to create one on the spot.

You don't need to use a Microsoft email address for this type of account and can use your current Gmail, Yahoo or AOL email etc. to create your account. You will also be prompted to create a password to go with this account and it doesn't have to be the same password you use for your email, but it can be if you want to keep things simple. Then you will use this password to log into your computer unless you configure a PIN for your login which I will be discussing in the next section.

Starting Up, Logging In, and Shutting Down

To be able to use your computer, obviously you will need to turn it on first. To do so, find the power button on the computer itself and press it once to start the power-up process. Depending on the speed of your computer this might take a minute or so.

Once your computer powers on, you will see a login screen with your name on it and it will ask you for your password or PIN. If it shows something like Owner for the name, that means that your computer was most likely preconfigured with a generic user before you bought it.

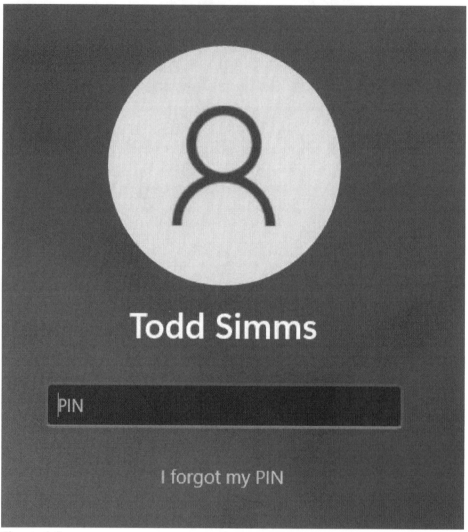

Figure 1.5

If your computer is asking for your password, you would then type it in, and press enter on the keyboard. If it's asking for a PIN, then you would do the same thing. One thing that might happen is you will first log in with a password and then Windows will ask you if you would like to configure a PIN to use instead of your password. This is an optional step so it's up to you to decide if you want to use a password or PIN to get into your computer.

While we are on the subject of the login screen, I want to show you a little trick that you might find useful. At the bottom right corner of the screen, you will see a few icons. The one at the far right that looks like a power button can be used to turn off your computer without having to log in. So if you ever turn on your computer and then realize you don't want to use it at the moment, you can click on this button to just shut it down.

Figure 1.6

Speaking of shutting down, it's very important that you shut down your computer properly to avoid damaging or corrupting any part of Windows or your other programs.

When shutting down, you need to do so from Windows, and not by pressing the power button on your computer. This should only be used to turn the computer on, not off.

You might run into a situation where your computer is frozen or not responding and you are unable to move your mouse or use your keyboard. When this happens, you might need to force the computer off. To do this, hold the power button down until the computer turns off. This should only be done if you have no other option!

To properly shut down your computer you will need to click on the Start button, then the power button and then click on the words *Shut down*. Figure 1.7 shows where each of these options are and in what order to click on them.

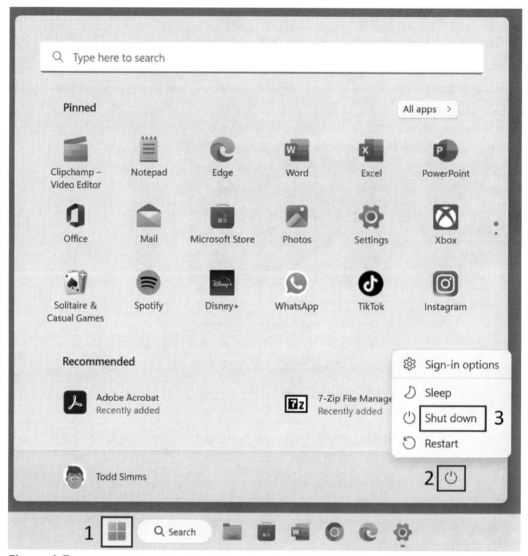

Figure 1.7

You might have noticed that there is also a *Sleep* and *Restart* option in step #3.

Sleep is used to put your computer in a semi powered off state to save electricity, but I never like to use this unless it's on a laptop that is running off the battery rather than being plugged into the wall.

Restart is used to shut down the computer and then restart it all in one step rather than you shutting it down and having to press the power button to turn it on again. You will usually do a restart after Windows does some updates or if you find your computer is running slow or giving you other issues.

 Restarting your computer is usually an effective way to get things working normally again when you find yourself having glitches or things are running slow. Just make sure you save anything you have been working on such as an email or document before restarting your computer.

Getting back to the shutdown procedure, once you click on Shut down, Windows will begin shutting itself down and then your computer will turn itself off automatically so there is no need to press the power button to complete the process.

One thing you should always do before shutting down or restarting your computer is close any programs that you might have open. This way everything gets shut down cleanly and you don't need to worry about having any issues the next time you turn on your computer.

Cortana
If you have a smartphone, then you might be familiar with the digital assistant that comes with them. For iPhones, you have Siri and for

Android phones, you have "Hey Google". You can then use these assistants to get directions, check the weather, make phone calls and so on.

Windows comes with its own assistant called Cortana and it works in a similar fashion, but I would say it's not quite as sophisticated as the assistant you get on your smartphone.

There are a couple of ways to open Cortana to start using it. If you click on the Start button or search icon, you can then type in Cortana in the search box to open it up.

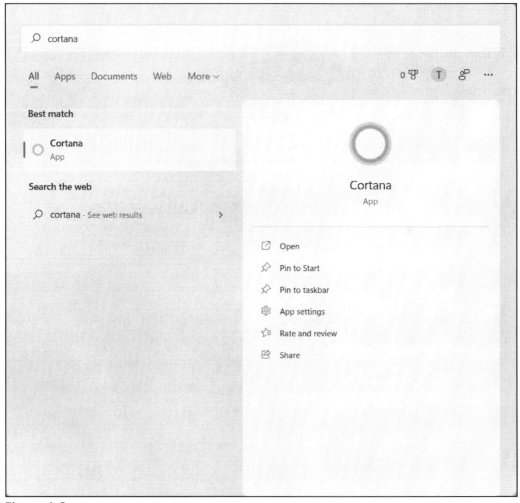

Figure 1.8

Or you can click on the Start button and then click on All apps and find Cortana in the list (figures 1.9 and 1.10).

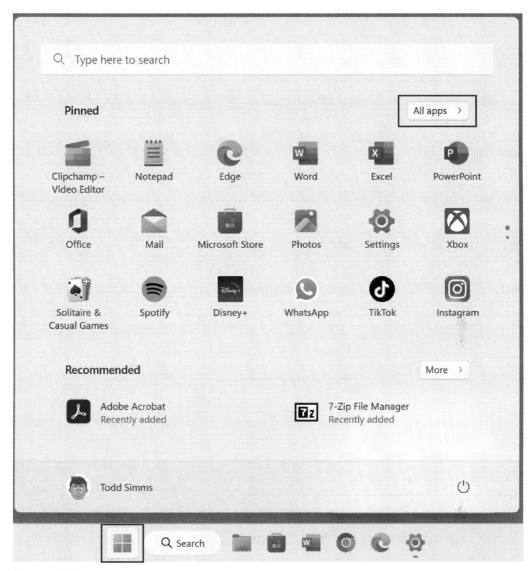

Figure 1.9

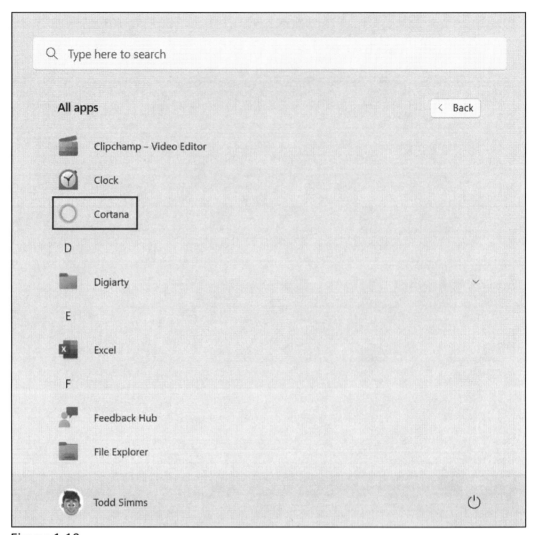

Figure 1.10

Once you start Cortana, you might be asked to sign in and you can use the same email address and password you use for your Microsoft account.

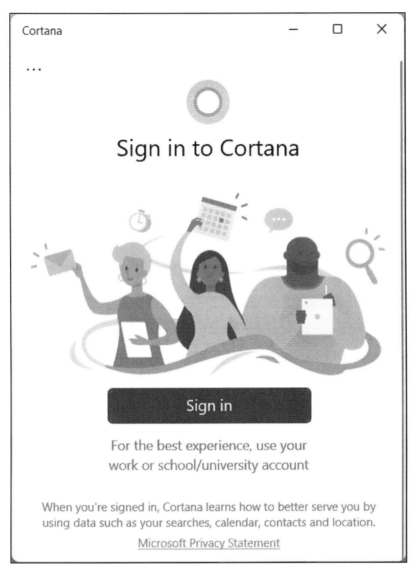

Figure 1.11

Once you are up and running you can use Cortana to get information for anything that you can normally search for online such as the weather, local restaurants, recipes, pictures and so on. Figures 1.12 through 1.14 show some examples of these types of results.

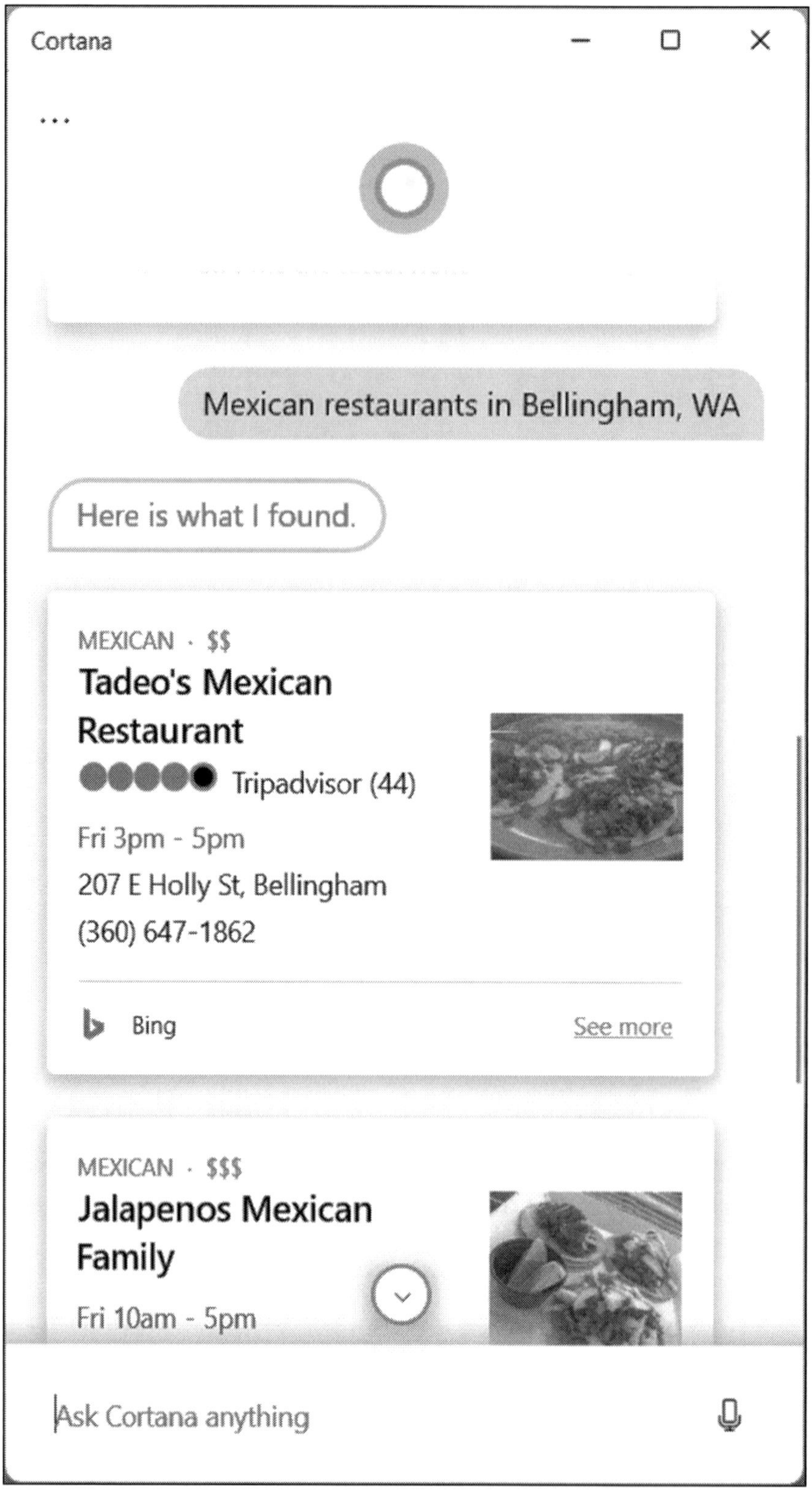

Cortana — ☐ ✕

· · ·

○

Mexican restaurants in Bellingham, WA

Here is what I found.

MEXICAN · $$

Tadeo's Mexican Restaurant

●●●●● Tripadvisor (44)

Fri 3pm - 5pm

207 E Holly St, Bellingham

(360) 647-1862

ᗷ Bing   See more

MEXICAN · $$$

Jalapenos Mexican Family

Fri 10am - 5pm   ⌄

Ask Cortana anything   🎤

Figure 1.12

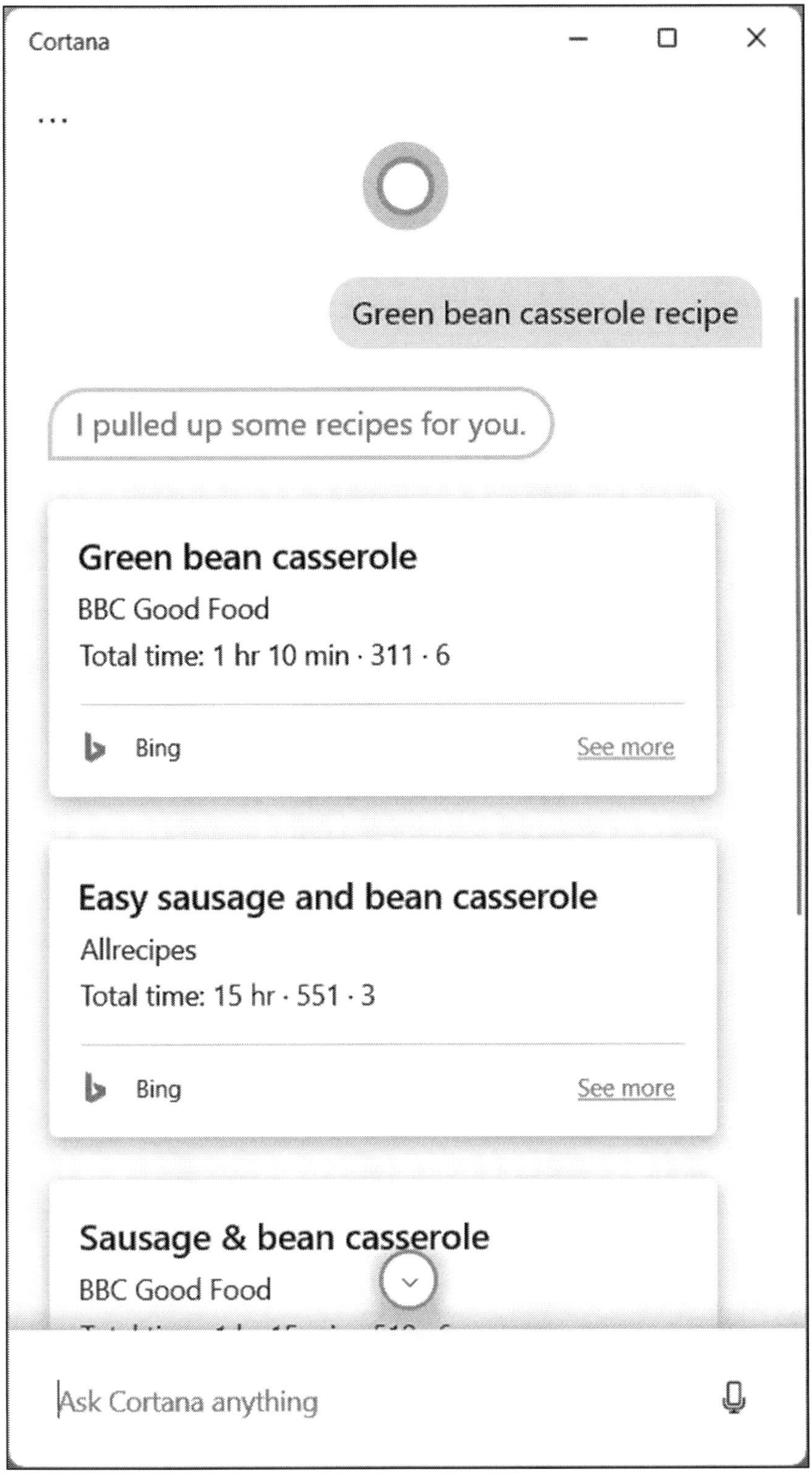
Cortana
Green bean casserole recipe
I pulled up some recipes for you.
Green bean casserole
BBC Good Food
Total time: 1 hr 10 min · 311 · 6
Bing
See more
Easy sausage and bean casserole
Allrecipes
Total time: 15 hr · 551 · 3
Bing
See more
Sausage & bean casserole
BBC Good Food
Ask Cortana anything

Figure 1.13

Cortana
...
show me pictures of Australian shepherds
I found this for you.
DOG BREED
Australian Shepherd
Scientific name: Canis lupus familiaris
Biological rank: Subspecies
Height: 1' 8" – 1' 11" (Asca standard, Male) · 1' 8" –...
Weight: 23 kg – 29 kg (Male) · 14 kg – 29 kg · 14 kg – 20 k...
Lifespan: 12 years – 18 years
Temperament: Active, Affectionate, Good-nature...
Bing
See more
Ask Cortana anything

Figure 1.14

Chapter 2 – Windows 11 Interface

Before getting too much further into working with Windows, I feel it is important to have an understanding of the components that make up the main Windows interface since that is what you will be working with every time you use your computer.

When it comes to being a proficient computer user, you really need to have a strong understanding of the basics in order to avoid getting frustrated while trying to complete even simple tasks.

For example, learning how to find files and folders on your hard drive is one of the most important things to know how to do since many tasks involve opening files, saving files and attaching files to emails etc. But at the same time, that is a more advanced area but I will be discussing this in chapter 4.

Windows Desktop
The main area that most people work from is called the desktop and it is named that because you can think of it as the top of your desk where you keep all of your files and paperwork that you commonly work with. But rather than paper files, you will find your digital files as well as icons that are used to open your programs such as your web browser or Microsoft Word for example.

Figure 2.1 shows a typical Windows 11 desktop with various icons, files and folders. You can have a variety of items on your desktop, and you can generally move these items around wherever you like by dragging them with your mouse and then releasing them in their new location. Of course your desktop icons will look different than mine because you will have different programs installed on your computer and different files on your desktop.

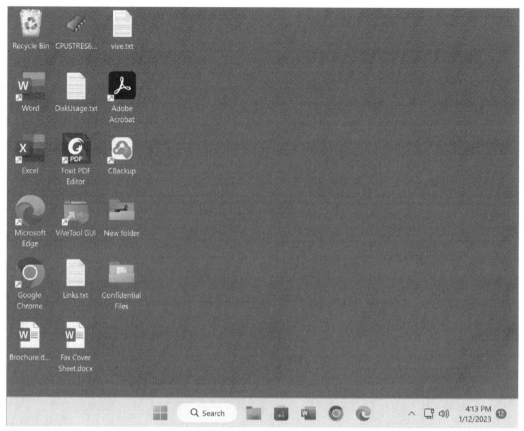

Figure 2.1

Figure 2.2 shows a closer view of these desktop items. Within figure 2.2, there are 4 types of items. The icons with the small arrow at the bottom left corner are shortcuts to programs such as Microsoft Word or the Edge and Google Chrome web browsers.

The 2 files at the bottom with the W on the icon are Microsoft Word documents and if you were to double click on one, it would open that document in the Word program.

The 2 folder icons represent folders that can contain files or even other folders, just like you can have on your physical desk itself. When you double click on a folder, it will open it up to show you what is inside as shown in figure 2.3 where I have the **Confidential Files** folder open to see its contents.

Figure 2.2

Figure 2.3

Finally, at the top left of figure 2.2, you will see the Windows Recycle Bin. When you delete a file or folder, it is placed in the Recycle Bin which is actually a folder itself. Then if you realize you didn't want to delete a particular file or folder, you can go into the Recycle Bin and restore it. I will be discussing the Recycle Bin in more detail in chapter 6.

When you install new software on your computer, often you will find that the software places a new icon (shortcut) on your desktop, making it easier to find and open the program.

You might have noticed that many people refer to software you install on your computer as either programs or apps. These terms can be used interchangeably for the most part even though there are some slight differences between the two which you really don't need to worry about.

I mentioned that you can drag these icons around on your desktop to rearrange them. You can also delete any files or icons you don't want on your desktop as well. Just be sure it's not something you need before deleting it though!

To delete a file or icon, simply click on it once to select it and then you can press the delete key (Del) on your keyboard to have it removed from your desktop. You can also right click on the item and then click on the trash can icon to delete it as well.

Many people like to save their documents, pictures and other types of files on their desktop since it's sometimes easier to see them rather than having to go to your Documents or Pictures folders. So when you save a file, you can look for the word *Desktop* on the left side of the window under This PC (figure 2.4), and when you click on that, whatever file you are saving or downloading etc. will be placed on your desktop.

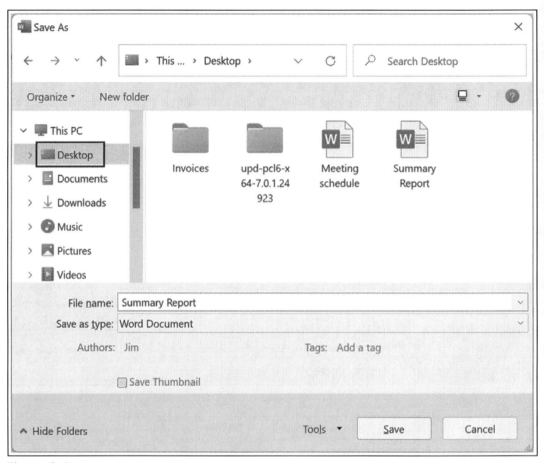

Figure 2.4

One last thing I want to mention about the desktop is that if you have a lot of programs open and want to get to your desktop quickly, you can use the Show Desktop button at the very bottom right hand corner of the screen.

Normally when you minimize an open program, you will click on the minimize symbol (-) at the top of that program's window as seen in figure 2.5. But if you have several programs open at the same time you might not want to click this symbol that many times.

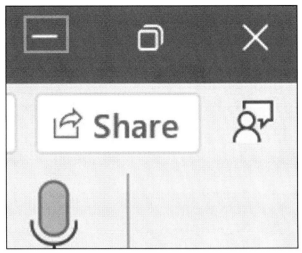

Figure 2.5

If you hover your mouse over at the very lower left corner of the screen, you will see a vertical bar that you can click on that will minimize (not close) any open programs you have running on your computer. You can also click it again to "maximize" the programs all at once.

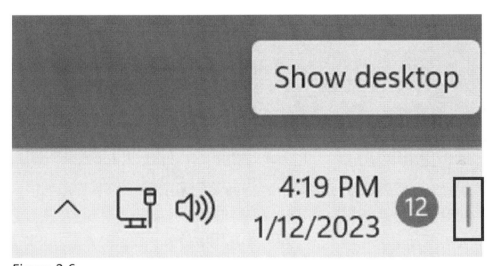

Figure 2.6

Taskbar

At the bottom of your computer screen you will see what is known as the Windows Taskbar. This is where you will find the Start Button (at the very left), the search tool, and various shortcut icons that can be used to open programs. The icons you have here will vary depending on your computer's configuration and what has been manually added and removed from the taskbar itself.

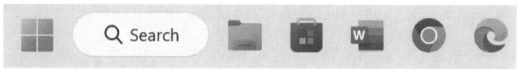

Figure 2.7

When you open a program using one of these shortcuts, the icon will change and will show a box around it with a blue bar underneath. If you look at the File Explorer shortcut (the folder icon) in figure 2.7 and then in figure 2.8, you can see how it changes when I open the File Explorer app.

Figure 2.8

When you open a program or app that is not on your taskbar, it will then add that program's icon to the taskbar showing you that it's open. If you compare the icons in figure 2.7 to figure 2.9, you will see that there is an extra one there at the far right now that I have opened the Microsoft Excel program. When you close the program, the icon will disappear from the taskbar if it's not attached or pinned to the taskbar to begin with.

Figure 2.9

You can unpin (remove) icons from the taskbar as well by right clicking on them and choosing *Unpin from taskbar*. I always like to remove any icons I don't use from the taskbar to clean things up and get some space back.

At the far right of the taskbar you will find what is known as the *notification area* or *system tray*, depending on who you talk to. Here you will find the date and time as well as icons that are used for certain programs that are running on your computer. It is possible for your computer to have programs or apps running in the background that you don't see but are necessary to keep your computer running properly.

Figure 2.10

If you click on the ^ symbol at the left side of the other icons, this will show you additional "hidden" icons for programs that are running in the background (figure 2.11).

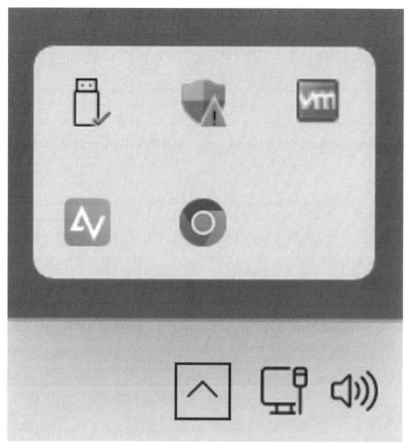

Figure 2.11

Going back to figure 2.10, you will see the number 12 in a circle, and this is the notification area, and this number indicates that I have 12 notifications. Most of the time, these notifications are used more for informational purposes, and you can just ignore them. But if you are curious as to what they are, you can click on that number, and you will then be shown the notifications as seen in figure 2.12.

Figure 2.12

Start Menu

Now that you know that the Start Menu is located on the taskbar, I would like to discuss what you will see on this menu and how to navigate around it.

You will use the Start Menu to open programs that you don't have shortcuts for on your desktop or on the Windows Taskbar. It's important to remember that the shortcuts on your desktop etc. are not the only programs that you have installed on your computer.

Figure 2.13 shows a typical Start Menu and of course what you see on your Start Menu will vary based on what programs you have installed on your computer and what files you have opened recently.

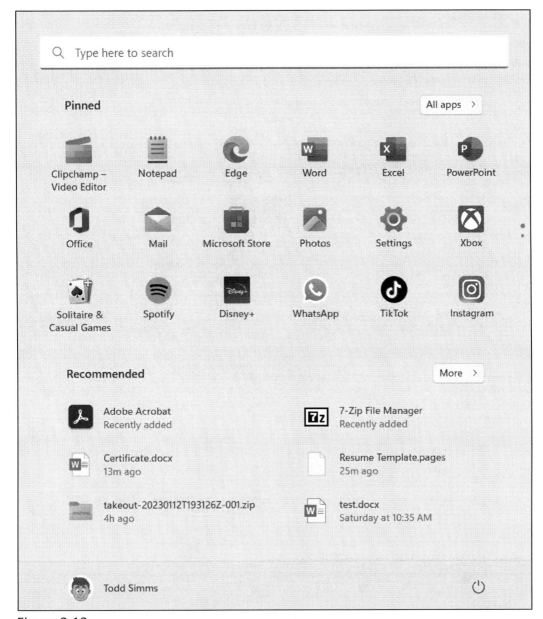

Figure 2.13

Here is a breakdown of the main sections of the Start Menu.

- **Search box** – This is the same search box you will get if you click the magnifying glass icon in the taskbar. You can use this to search for files, apps, settings, documents, information online and more. When you click within the search box, it will change to a search

- screen as seen in figure 2.14, showing you your recent searches and offering suggestions that for subjects that you might be interested in online.

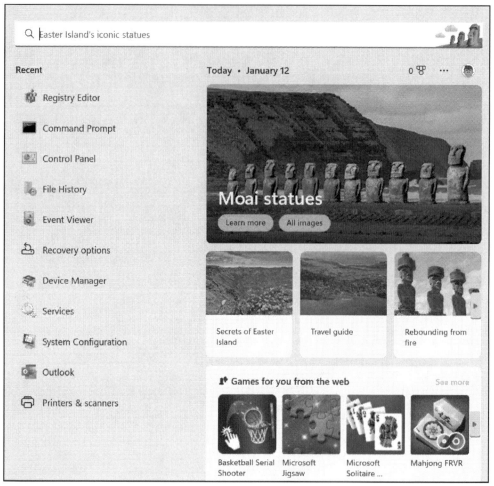

Figure 2.14

- **Pinned** – Here you will find programs and apps that have been pinned to the Start Menu, meaning they have been placed there for quick access purposes. You can unpin items from here as well as pin your own items by right clicking on them and choosing *Pin to Start Menu*. The two small dots to the right of the Xbox icon are used to move to the next page of pinned items.

- **All apps button** - This will show you an alphabetical listing of all the programs and apps you have installed on your computer. You can then open any one of them just by clicking on its icon from the list. You can use the up and down arrows to scroll through this list of programs.

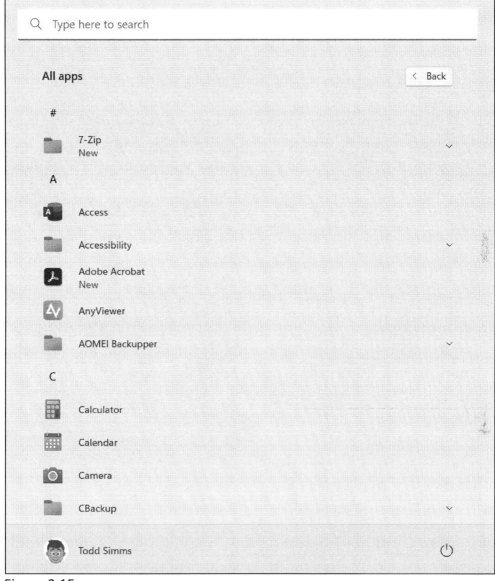

Figure 2.15

- **Recommended** – Here you will find programs that Windows thinks you might be interested in using as well as recent documents and other files you have opened in case you want to quickly access them again.

- **User account information** – Clicking on your username (Todd Simms in my case), will give you the option to log out of the computer, lock the computer or change your user account settings such as your password etc.

- **Power options** – I have already discussed this area but once again, it is where you will go to shut down or restart your computer.

Searching for Apps in the Microsoft Store

If you have a smartphone, then you might be familiar with the process of installing apps from the App Store (iPhone) or Play Store (Android) to add additional functionality to your phone or even to just have some fun by installing a game.

Starting with Windows 8, Microsoft introduced the Microsoft Store as a place you can go to download and install free and pay for apps and games as well as stream movies and TV shows. You might have the Microsoft Store icon on your taskbar and if not, you can find it on your Start Menu.

Figure 2.16

Once you open the Microsoft Store app, you will be shown some of the more popular apps, games and movies etc. At the top of the window, there will be a search box, and on the left side you will have various categories such as apps, gaming and films & TV.

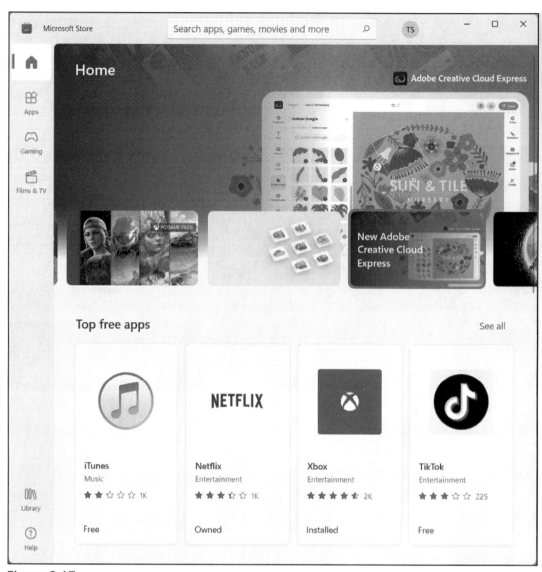

Figure 2.17

If you want to find a particular type of app or game, you can type your search term in the search box and press enter on your keyboard. Figure 2.18 shows what happens if I search for the game **Scrabble**.

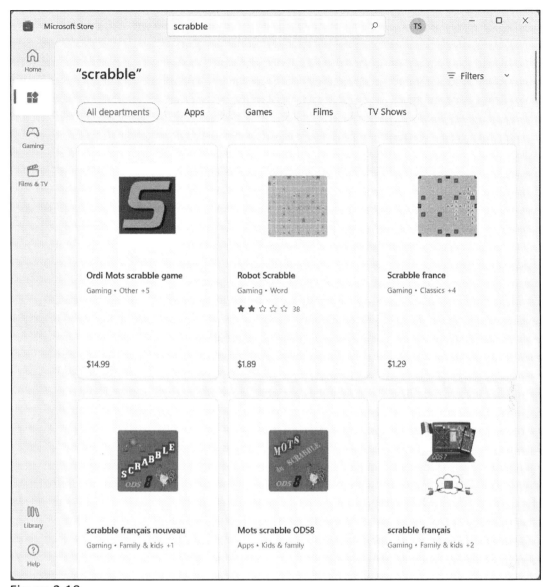

Figure 2.18

Once I perform my search, I will be shown various results and some of the apps will be free while others will cost money. If I were to click on the word *Filters* at the top right, I would have the ability to only show free apps if that is only what I wish to see.

Once I find an app I would like to install on my computer, I can click on it to bring up the information screen as seen in figure 2.19.

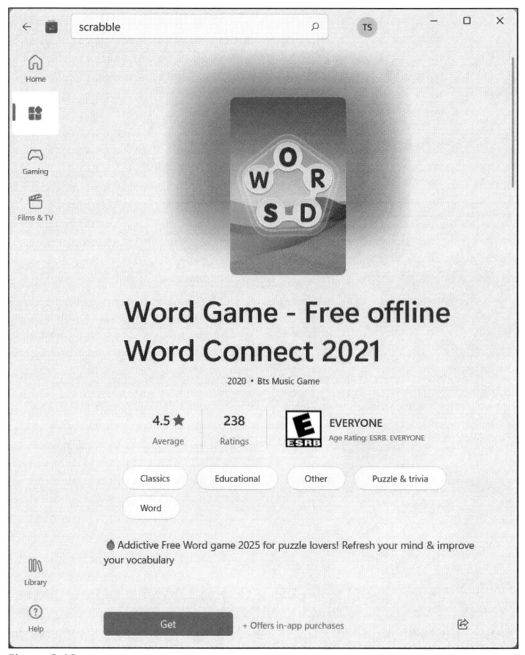

Figure 2.19

Here you can see the publisher's name, check out the average rating and number of reviews as well as see things like screenshots and a description of the app (figure 2.20).

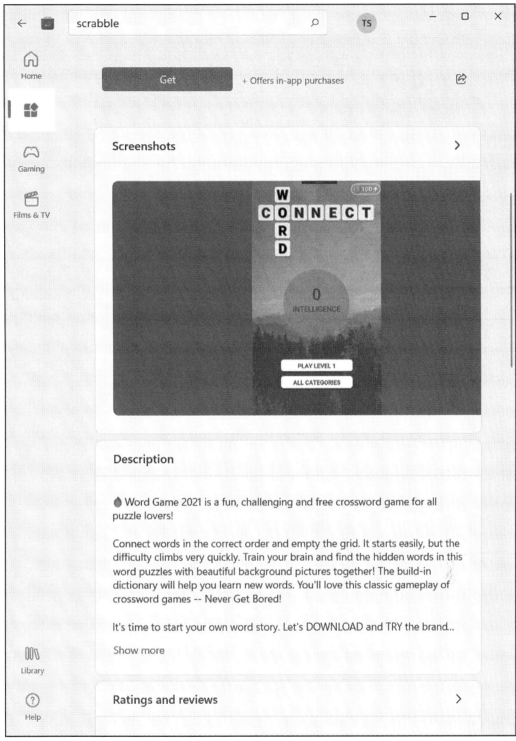

Figure 2.20

If you like what you see, you can click on the *Get* button to download the app and have it installed on your computer.

When installing free apps, keep in mind that they are free for a reason. And this is usually because they will have advertisements within the app, or they want to try and convince you to buy the "better" version that has more features.

Once the installation is complete, the Get button will change to something that says Play or Open and you can click on this to start using the app. You will also be able to find it on your Start Menu under *All apps* or in the *Recommended* section since it's a new app.

If you find an app that you like that is not free, then you will need to set up a payment method in order to purchase the app. For the most part, you can usually find a free app that does the job just fine.

Installing Software
The Microsoft Store is not the only way to add new software to your computer. Sometimes you might want to install some other software such as Microsoft Word or a game that you have on a CD.

The process for installing software can vary depending on what you are trying to install and on what media the software resides. You can have software on a CD, USB flash drive, or even have it be a file that you downloaded from the internet.

You might never need to install software on your computer if you use it for just the basics and it already came with everything you need. But there might come a time when you want to try some new software or need some additional software to accomplish a specific task. Sure you can have someone install it for you, or you can try to install it yourself.

The process of installing software in Windows is fairly simple. If you are installing it from a CD, the installation procedure should start when you insert the CD into your CD\DVD drive. Or if you downloaded an installation file from the internet, you can start the procedure by simply double clicking the file you downloaded.

For my example, I have downloaded a program called 7 Zip which is used for making zip files in case you know what those are. If you don't, then it doesn't matter for this demonstration. Also keep in mind that the process will vary and also look a little different for other software titles.

To install the 7 Zip program, I will find the file I downloaded and double click on it to start the installation process.

7z2107-x64.exe

Figure 2.21

Windows will then ask me if I trust this program and want to continue with the installation and I will click on the Yes button.

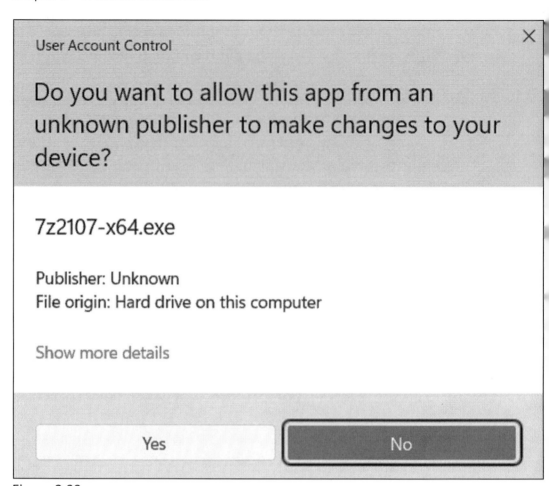

User Account Control   ×

Do you want to allow this app from an
unknown publisher to make changes to your
device?

7z2107-x64.exe

Publisher: Unknown
File origin: Hard drive on this computer

Show more details

Yes   No

Figure 2.22

I will now be prompted to specify where on my computer I want to
install the program. 99% of the time, you can simply go with what the
software suggests and click on *Install*.

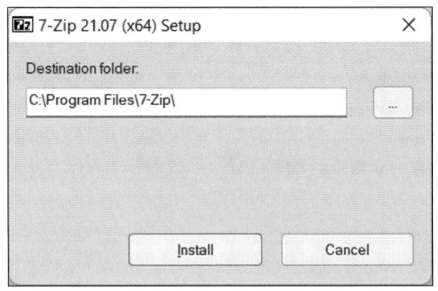

Figure 2.23

Then the installation will proceed and when it's finished you will be notified.

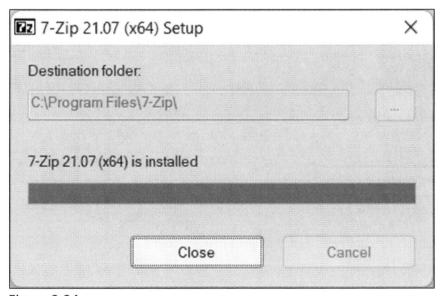

Figure 2.24

There may be additional steps such as accepting a license agreement etc. but for the most part, it's a matter of clicking next a few times until the process is complete. Then you will have your new program shortcut on your Start Menu or maybe even on your desktop.

Right Clicking Options

When using computers, we tend to rely on our mouse to help us navigate and click on items to do what we need to do. Sure you can use a computer without a mouse, but it tends to be a bit more cumbersome.

You might have noticed that your mouse comes with two buttons and a scroll wheel in the middle. The scroll wheel can be used to scroll up and down on documents and web pages without having to use the scroll bars that you find on the right side of the screen.

One thing you might want to try on your computer is to use the arrow keys over on the right side of the keyboard. Sometimes these can be easier to use when you need to scroll up and down on a page or even move your mouse cursor to the left or to the right. Give it a try!

Using the right button on your mouse can open up a whole other world of options when it comes to using Windows. And when I say the right button, I mean the one on the right!

Depending on what you right click on, you will get a variety of different tools and options. Figure 2.25 shows what you can do when you right click on your desktop. Here you can do things such as change your screen resolution or go to the personalization settings where you can change your desktop background image etc. The *New* selection will let you create a new folder as well as various types of files.

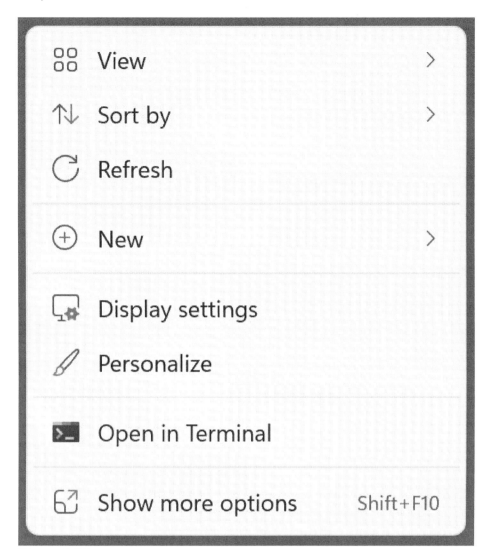

Figure 2.25

Figure 2.26 shows what you can do when you right click on a folder. At the bottom of the menu you have your options for cut, copy and paste and if you recall, I mentioned you can pin items to your taskbar and Start Menu, and this is one way to do so.

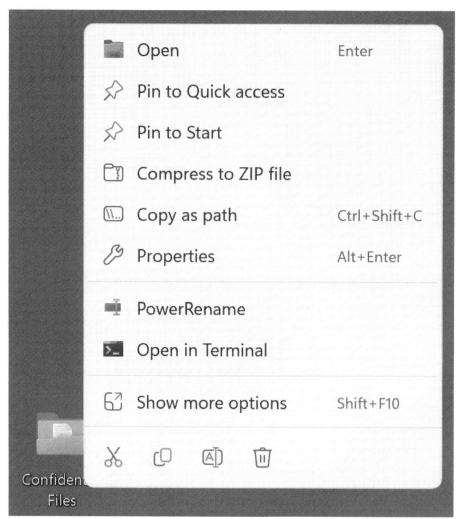

Figure 2.26

Figure 2.27 shows all the options you get when right clicking on the Start Button. Even though these are more advanced options, I just wanted to show you that you can right click on almost anything to get yourself a quick way to change options or take an action on that item.

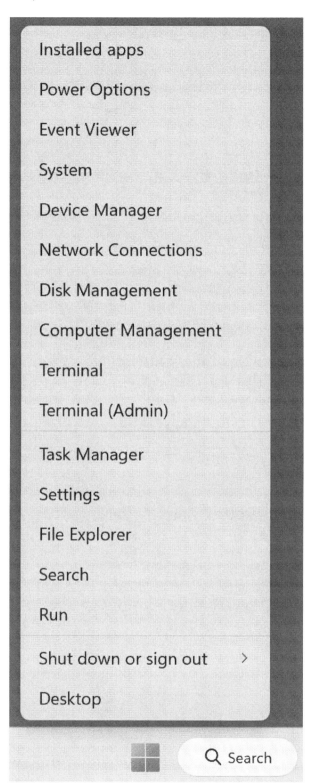

Figure 2.27

Chapter 3 – Customizing Windows

Once you start using your computer for a while, you might start to wish there were easier ways to do things or maybe a way to make your computer fit your style a little more regarding its appearance.

Fortunately, Windows has always been customizable, and Windows 11 is no different. Once you learn how to change some of the basic Windows configurations, you will find that your computer will be easier to use and also more pleasant to work with.

Creating Desktop Shortcuts
In the last chapter, I discussed the Windows desktop and mentioned how it's most likely going to be the main area you will be working with while using your computer. Most people like to have the icons/shortcuts that they use the most on their desktop for easy access. But what if you are missing shortcuts to your favorite programs on your desktop?

Fortunately, it's very easy to add new shortcuts to your desktop so you will have an easy way to find what you are looking for. Shortcuts are not only used for programs but also for files and folders.

To create a desktop icon for a program, you will need to click on the Start button and then click on the *All apps* button to show the alphabetical listing of all the programs installed on your computer. Then once you find the app you want to add to your desktop, simply click and drag it to a spot on your desktop and release the mouse button as seen in figure 3.1.

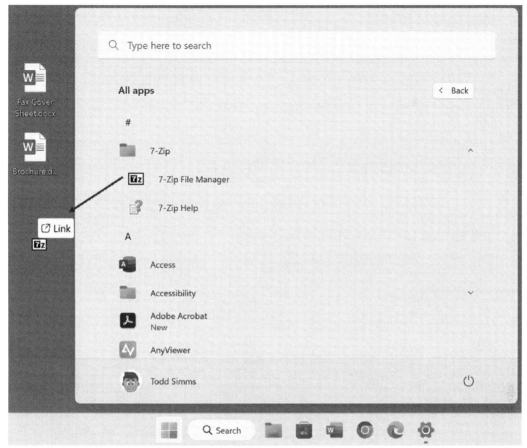

Figure 3.1

You will most likely see the word Link appear as you are dragging it but that is ok. Then once you let go of the mouse button, your new shortcut icon will be on the desktop.

Creating shortcuts for files and folders works a little differently and you need to make sure that you do the process correctly, otherwise you will be copying these items to your desktop rather than making a shortcut.

Then you will have the issue of having duplicate files or folders on your computer.

To create a shortcut for a file or folder, simply right click on that file or folder and then click on the *Copy* button.

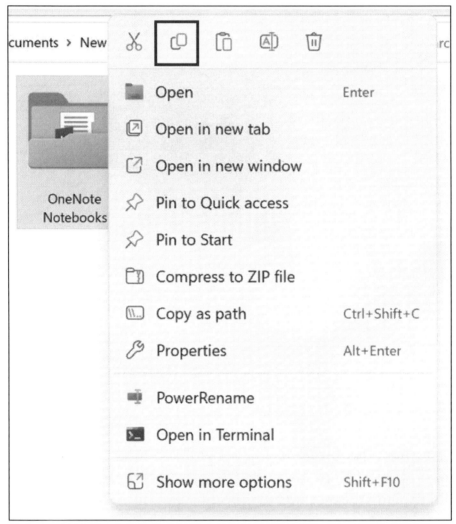

Figure 3.2

Now you can go to your desktop and right click on any blank area and choose *Paste shortcut*, which is different than clicking on the Paste button at the top of the menu.

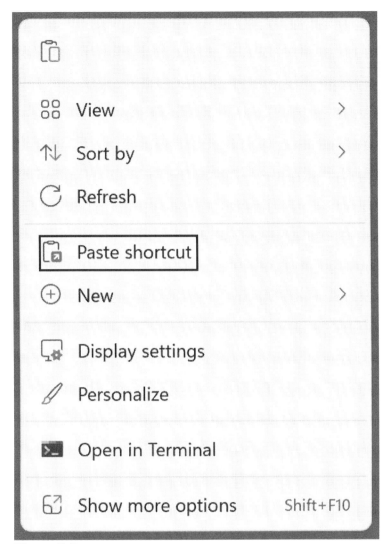

Figure 3.3

The difference between paste and paste shortcut is that paste will make a copy of the file or folder while paste shortcut will just make an icon that you can click on which will open the original file or folder from its actual location.

After you paste your shortcut, it will create the file or folder with the same name but will put – **Shortcut** after it, indicating that it is a shortcut to the item and not the item itself. It will also add an arrow icon to the lower left corner of the file or folder itself.

OneNote Notebooks - Shortcut

Figure 3.4

One very important thing to remember about shortcuts is that if you delete them, you are only deleting the icon and not the program, file, or folder itself so the original will still be there. You should always be aware of what you are deleting before you delete it.

Changing Your Desktop Background
Since you will be working with your Windows desktop for many of your tasks, it makes sense that you might want a background image that was nice to look at. Depending on what brand your computer is, they might add their own background image or leave the default Windows Bloom background as seen in figure 3.5.

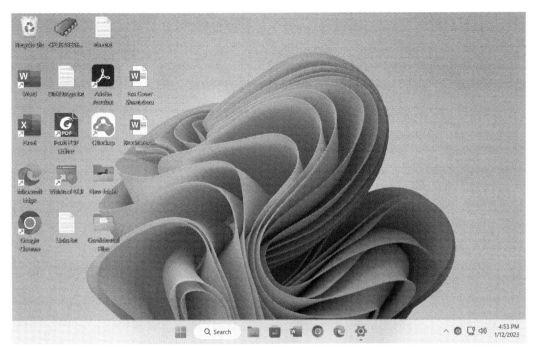

Figure 3.5

Windows does come with some default background pictures that you can use if you do not like the one that is currently in use on your desktop.

There are a couple of ways to get to the settings where you can change the picture, but I like to right click on a blank area of the desktop and choose the *Personalize* option. At the top you will have some themes to choose from that will change the background picture, as well as the general colors used for Windows (figure 3.6).

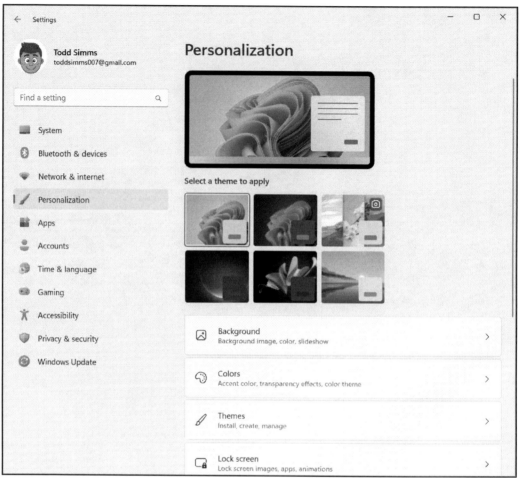

Figure 3.6

If you click on the *Background* section, you can then choose a different picture or even go with a solid color instead of a photo. If you want to use a personal picture that you have on your computer, you can click on the *Browse photos* button and find it on your hard drive and then set it to be your background image.

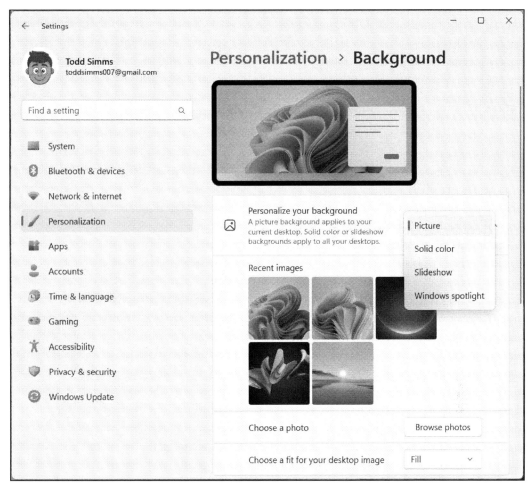

Figure 3.7

Where it says *Choose a fit for your desktop image*, this will allow you to change how the picture is formatted for your computer. The default selection is *fill* but you can choose from other options such as center, stretch, span and so on. You can choose the different options to get a preview of how it will look before selecting one.

If a single picture or solid color is not what you are looking for, then you can choose the *Slideshow* option which will take photos from a folder of your choosing and display them as your background image. They will then be cycled through at an interval you specify as if they were part of an actual slideshow.

Figure 3.8 shows how my desktop looks after applying a photo I had of a beach on my hard drive. As you can see, it's much more pleasant to look at!

Figure 3.8

 When choosing a custom picture for your background, you should make sure that it is not so "busy" that it makes it hard to see your icons on top of it. You can also try to move the icons to other locations on the screen where you can see them better.

Changing Your Display Settings

Your computer and monitor are capable of using many different resolution settings allowing you to find the setting that works the best for your eyesight. You can change this resolution to make things bigger or smaller on the screen as needed.

When you lower the resolution, things become larger, but you can't fit as much on the screen without having to scroll more down a page etc. With a higher resolution, things appear smaller, and you can fit more on the screen. Higher resolutions will also result in a crisper, clearer image. You can think of it as comparing your current 4k TV to the older tube style TVs that were around before flat screens.

When you buy a new computer and monitor, they are generally set at the highest resolution the monitor will support. This is fine for most people, but it might be too small for you. If this is the case, then it's very easy to change.

The easiest way to get to your display settings is to right click on a blank area of the desktop and then choose *Display settings*.

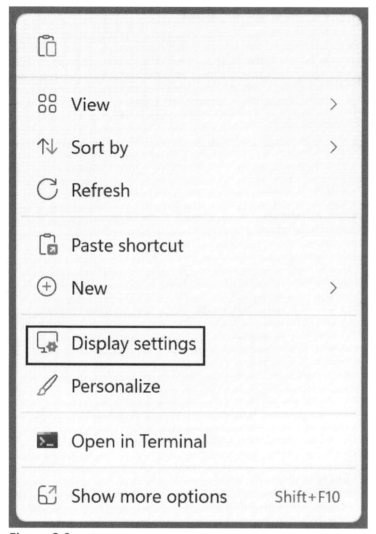

Figure 3.9

From here, you will have two places that you can make adjustments to in order to change how everything appears on the screen in regard to its size.

You might first want to increase the scale size from the default 100% to a higher number. This often makes things easier to see without needing to adjust the resolution settings.

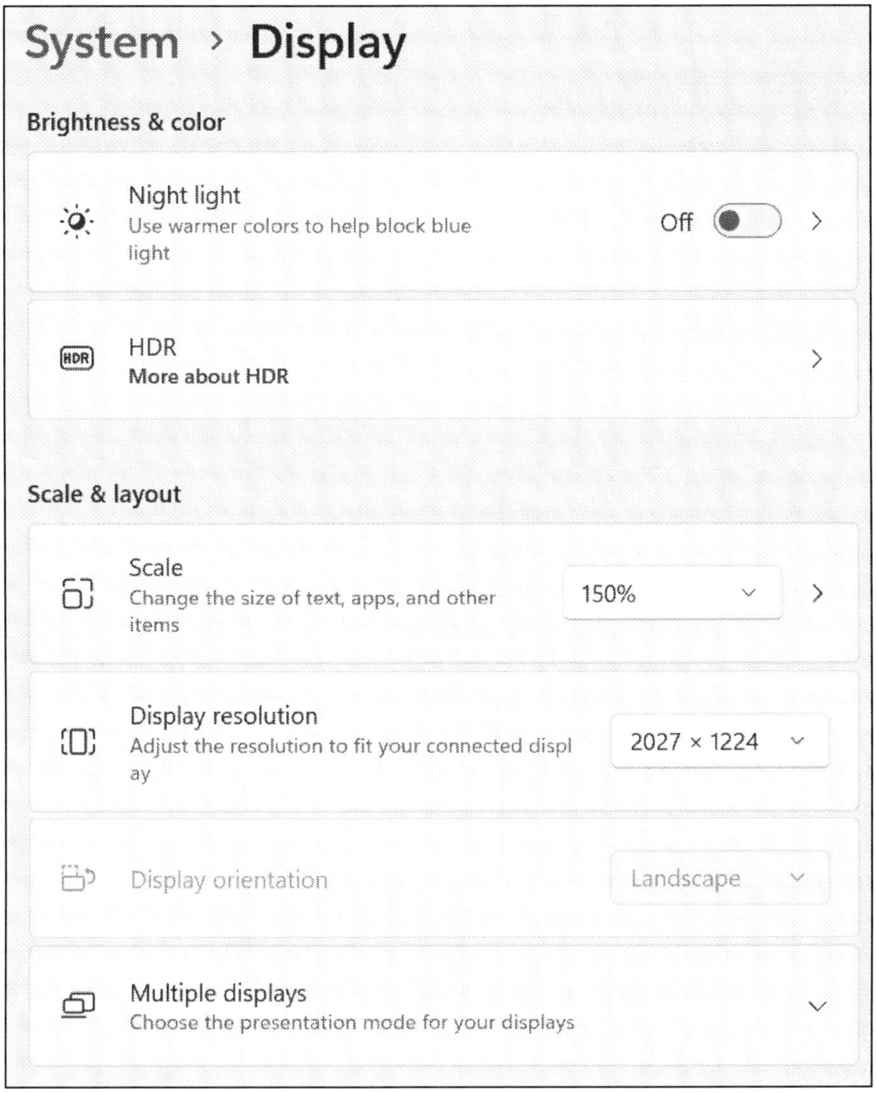

System > Display

Brightness & color

☀	**Night light** Use warmer colors to help block blue light	Off ⬤	>
HDR	**HDR** More about HDR		>

Scale & layout

⊡	**Scale** Change the size of text, apps, and other items	150% ∨	>
⊡	**Display resolution** Adjust the resolution to fit your connected display	2027 × 1224 ∨	
⊟	Display orientation	Landscape ∨	
⊡	**Multiple displays** Choose the presentation mode for your displays		∨

Figure 3.10

If that doesn't work, you can try a lower resolution from the *Display resolution* setting to make things larger on the screen. When you choose a different setting, it will change instantly, and you will be given the option to keep or revert the changes. If you don't choose one of the selections as seen in figure 3.11, Windows will automatically revert back to your previous resolution.

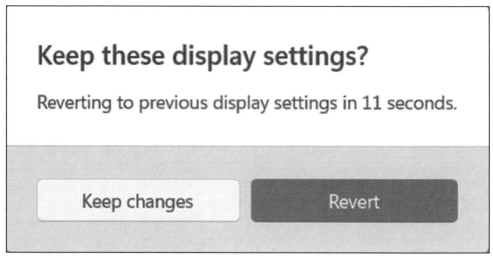

Figure 3.11

You can play with these settings until you find the one that works best for you. Just keep in mind that some of the settings will cause your display to not take up the entire size of the monitor so you will be losing screen space if you use certain resolutions. I would also make a note of your original setting in case you need to go back to it.

Pinning Items to the Start Menu and Taskbar
Now that you know how to add a shortcut to your desktop to allow for quick access to a program, you might also want to know how you can do the same for your Start Menu and taskbar. This way you can have several ways to open a program and not just be restricted to your desktop shortcut.

It is very easy to add a program icon to the Start Menu or taskbar but the process for doing so is not the same as it is for adding a shortcut to the desktop and is actually a little easier. The one thing that you need to be aware of is what items you can pin to the Start Menu and what items you can pin to the taskbar.

The process of pinning an item is fairly easy and all you need to do is right click on that item and choose either *Pin to Start* or *Pin to Taskbar*.

But you will notice that sometimes you only have the option to do one or the other.

Figure 3.12 shows that you only have the Pin to Start option when right clicking an item on the desktop.

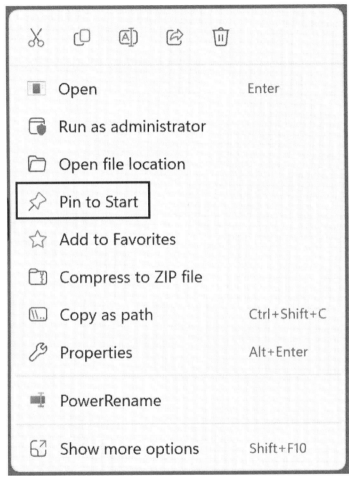

	Open	Enter
Run as administrator	
Open file location	
Pin to Start	
Add to Favorites	
Compress to ZIP file	
Copy as path	Ctrl+Shift+C
Properties	Alt+Enter
PowerRename	
Show more options	Shift+F10

Figure 3.12

So if you want to pin an item to your taskbar, all you need to do is click on *Start* and then on the *All apps* button. Then you can find the program in the list and then right click it and choose *More* and then *Pin to taskbar* as shown in figure 3.13.

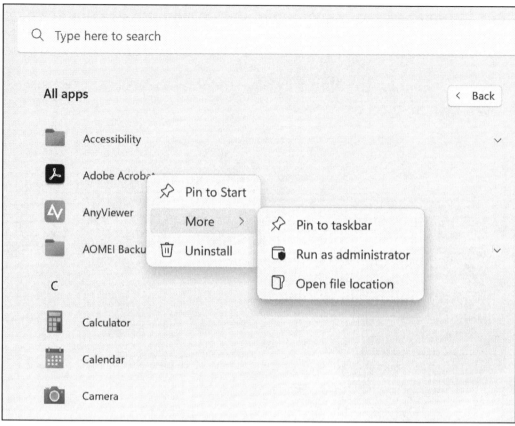

Figure 3.13

Figure 3.14 shows my taskbar before pinning the Adobe Acrobat program to it and figure 3.15 shows it after.

Figure 3.14

Figure 3.15

With newer builds of Windows 11, you can drag and drop your program shortcuts on to the taskbar to have them pinned. Simply drag them to a spot on the taskbar and then click on Link when it appears.

If you choose the Pin to Start option when right clicking on an item, then it will appear in the *Pinned* section of your Start Menu when you click on the Start button. As you can see in figure 3.16, my Adobe Acrobat icon is pinned to my Start Menu for easy access. If it gets pinned on the second page of your apps, simply right click the icon and choose *Move to front* to have it be the first app on the Pinned list.

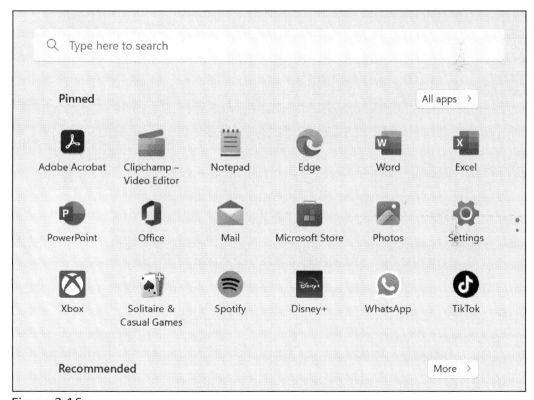

Figure 3.16

Screen Savers

Screen savers have been around since the beginning of Windows, and they really haven't changed too much in the way they look or function.

Screen savers are not as popular as they used to be thanks to improvements in monitor technology that helps prevent them from being damaged by having the same image on the screen for long periods of time.

But if you are the type who prefers to use one, then they are still an option in Windows 11, but you won't have any modern, up to date screen savers to choose from.

The screen saver settings are in a rather odd place within your Windows settings, but you can get to it the same way you changed your desktop background by right clicking on a blank area of the desktop and then choosing *Personalize*.

Then you can click on the *Lock screen* section and finally on the *Screen saver* section. This will open the screen saver configuration box which has stayed about the same since the beginning of Windows.

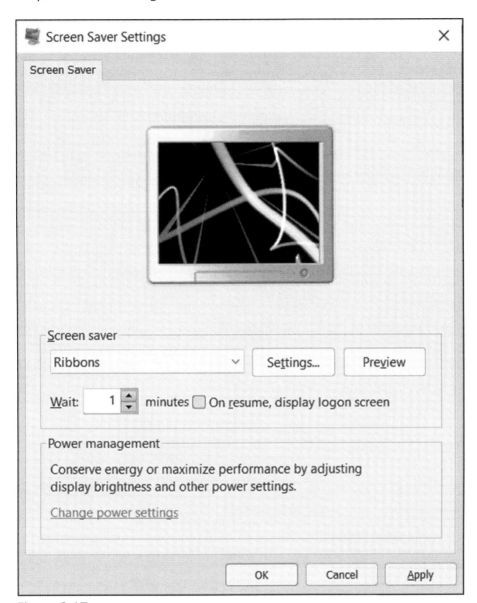

Figure 3.17

Now you can choose one of the screen saver types and then select how many minutes you want to wait before it activates or turns on. This time setting starts when you stop touching your mouse or keyboard and every time you touch one of them again, it resets the timer.

One thing you might want to do rather than use a screen saver is have Windows turn off your monitor after a set period of time instead. You can get to these settings by clicking on the *Change power settings* link at the bottom of figure 3.17. Then you can click on Choose when to turn off the display.

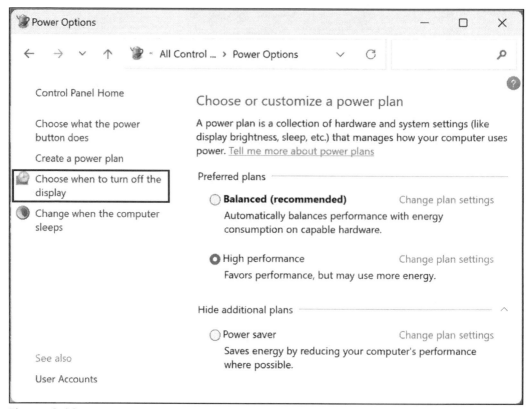

Figure 3.18

Then you can choose a time interval that you would like to use from the dropdown list where it says *Turn off the display*.

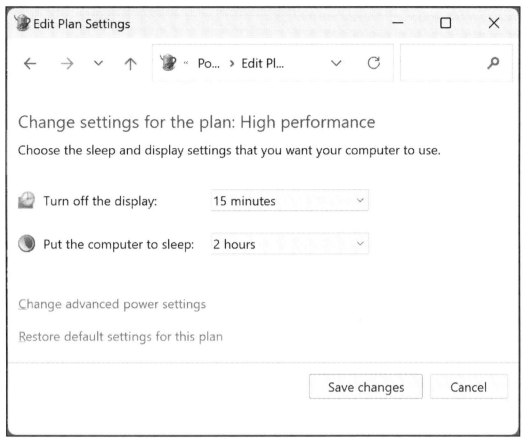

Figure 3.19

You can also get to these settings from the Windows settings app which I have been using to show you most of these other settings throughout this book. You can get to the Windows settings from the Start Menu by clicking on the Settings icon.

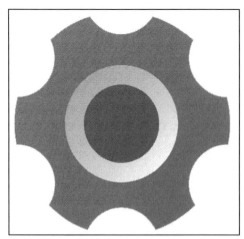

Figure 3.20

You will notice how the screen looks different, but the settings are the same. This is just a case of having more than one way to do something within Windows.

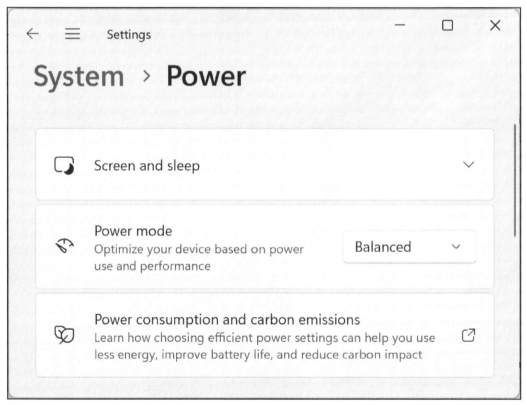

Figure 3.21

Even though Microsoft has been updating Windows with each new version, they tend to leave many of the old tools and settings in place so seasoned Windows users can still use the tools they are used to. I'm sure eventually these old tools will be removed from Windows altogether.

Chapter 4 – Managing Your Files

Hopefully as you have been reading through the first 3 chapters of this book, you were not getting too confused but unfortunately you cannot make a book about computers that is as easy to understand as a kindergarten textbook!

This chapter may or may not be the most confusing chapter in the book but it's one of the most important since being able to manage your files and folders is essential if you want to be a proficient computer user. You might have noticed how often you need to access a file or folder when doing things such as opening a document, viewing a photo or attaching a file to an email.

The Windows File and Folder Structure
The most important thing to know when it comes to managing your files and folders is now to find them. I will be discussing how to search for files later in the chapter but want to begin with how the Windows file structure works.

You can think of your computer as a file cabinet and your files and folders as actual paper files and folders stored within it. You can have a folder called **Receipts** and then have several paper receipts within that folder. And you might even have a folder within the receipts folder called **Home repair receipts**. This is known as a subfolder and is demonstrated in figure 4.1.

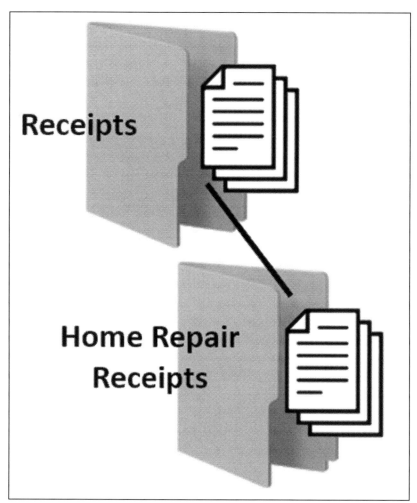

Figure 4.1

Figure 4.2 shows a more complex illustration of folders and subfolders. No matter how many folders and subfolders you have, there will always be a root folder where everything branches off of.

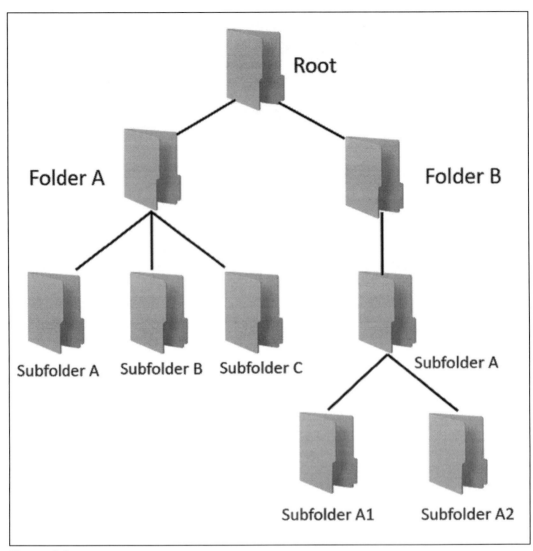

Figure 4.2

Figure 4.3 shows the folder structure on a typical Windows computer. Each **V** symbol indicates that is an open subfolder of a folder above it. As you can see, you can have many upon many folders and subfolders on your computer. Plus most of these folders contain files that are not even shown in the graphic!

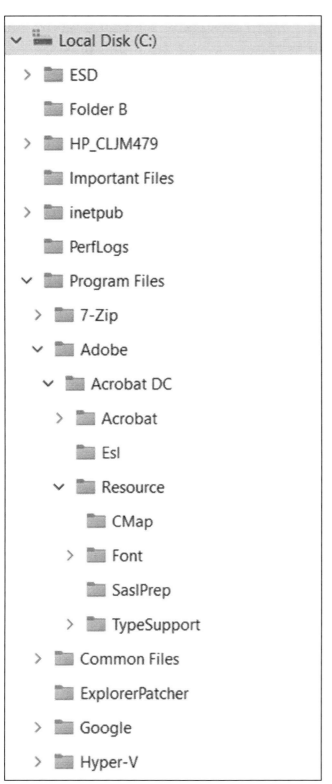

Figure 4.3

The way you view your files and folders is by using the *File Explorer* program that comes built into Windows. You can find it on your Start Menu under All apps. What you see in File Explorer will vary since not all computers have the same files and folders. Figure 4.4 shows a typical Windows File Explorer screen. On the left side of the window, you will have the folder tree like you saw in figure 4.3.

To the right, you will see the details of whatever folder you have open on the left. So in figure 4.4, **This PC** is selected on the left, and it shows the contents of the PC which includes the default Windows folders (discussed next) and the hard drives and CD\DVD drive on the right.

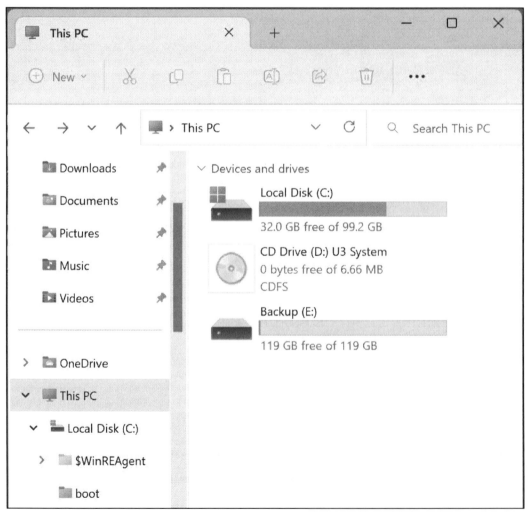

Figure 4.4

If I were to click on *Pictures* on the left, I would be shown the contents of the Pictures folder on the right as seen in figure 4.5. As you can see, the Pictures folder contains both files and other folders.

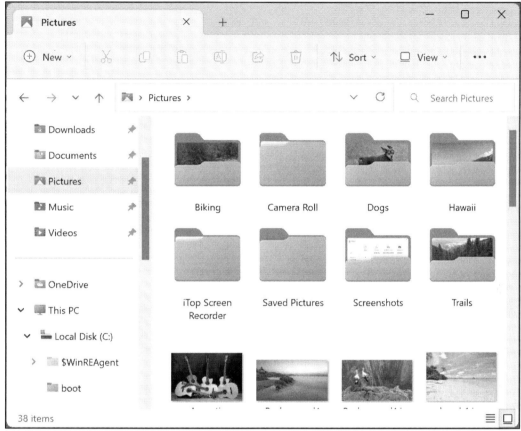

Figure 4.5

Then if I were to double click on the Hawaii folder for example, I would then be shown its contents as seen in figure 4.6.

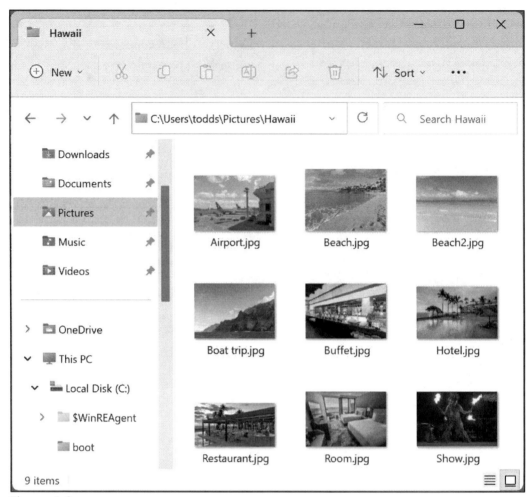

Figure 4.6

To navigate back to where I was before, I can click on the back arrow at the upper left corner of the window, just like I would with my web browser to go back to the previous page.

It would be a good idea to open File Explorer and just start poking around your files and folders just to get a better idea of how everything is organized. You don't need to remember where anything is necessarily but it's good practice to know how to move around the app.

Windows Default Folders

One nice thing about Windows is that you can place your files such as documents and photos into whatever folders you like, or even create your own folders for these items.

However, Windows does come with some default folders that are meant to be used to store certain types of files to help keep you organized. Figure 4.7 shows these default folders and you can tell by the names of these folders, what types of files are meant to be stored in them.

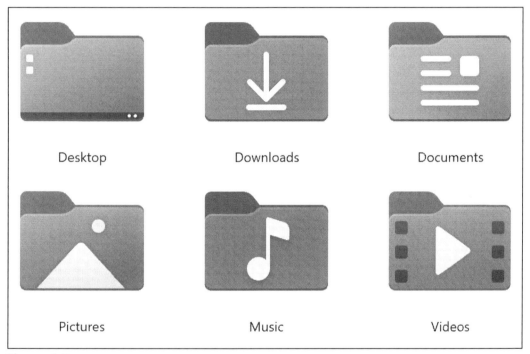

Desktop   Downloads   Documents

Pictures   Music   Videos

Figure 4.7

You might have noticed for example that when you save a document when working in Microsoft Word that it defaults to your *Documents* folder. This is set up this way on purpose to help you keep all your files in the same place to keep things organized.

You might have also noticed that when you download a file from the internet that it goes into your *Downloads* folder. Once again, this is

81

meant to make it easier on you so you can just go to one place to see all your files.

You don't need to use these default folders if you would like to keep your files elsewhere but if you don't have a reason to change this behavior, then it's a good idea to just use them.

And just like with any other folder, you can right click one of these default folders and have it pinned to your Start Menu or drag it to your desktop to create a shortcut.

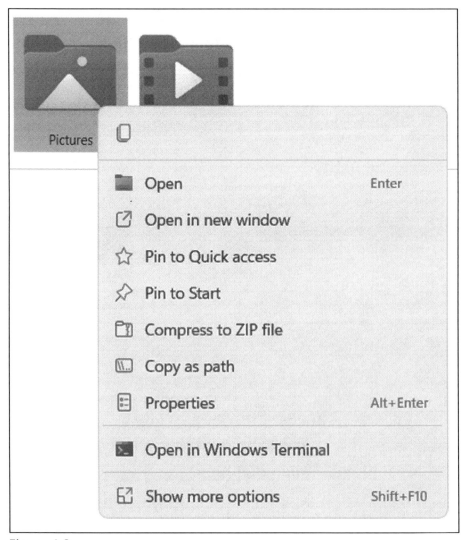

Figure 4.8

You might be wondering what the *Pin to Quick access* option is used for. This is a section at the top right of File Explorer that you can use to pin folders that you often use. Think of it as working the same way bookmarks or favorites work in your web browser. This was actually called Quick access for years but has recently been changed to Home even though the right click option still says Pin to Quick access, but this might change to Pin to Home eventually.

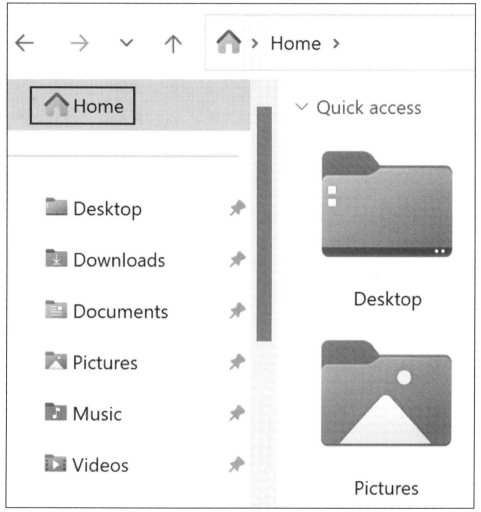

Figure 4.9

Searching for Files and Folders

There will most likely be a time when you need to access a file or folder such as a document or picture and don't remember where it is located on your computer. Fortunately, you can do a search for these items assuming you know their name or at least part of their name.

You can search for files and folders from the search icon on the taskbar, but I like to open File Explorer and search from there. At the top right of the window, you will see a search box where you can type your search word or words.

One thing to make a note of is that Windows will search for your word in the folder that you have selected so make sure you are in the right place first.

Figure 4.10 shows that *This PC* is selected on the left so therefore the search box says at the upper right says *Search This PC*. This means it will search your entire computer rather than a specific folder which is what you want if you have no idea where your file or folder is located.

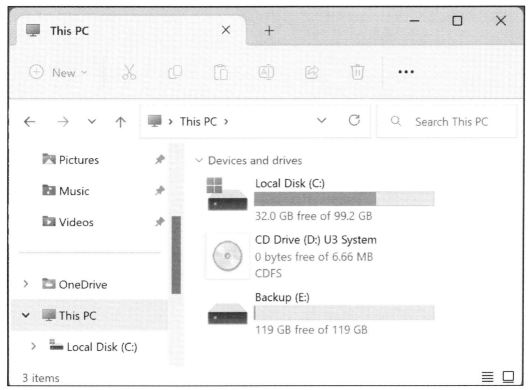

Figure 4.10

Figure 4.11 says *Search Documents* since the Documents folder is selected on the left.

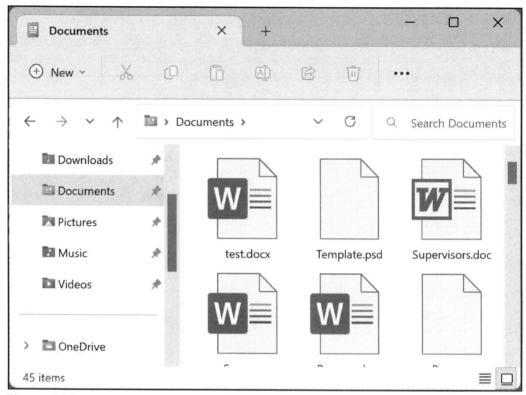

Figure 4.11

I will now search my entire computer (This PC) for anything with Hawaii in the name. As you can see in figure 4.12, it found folders called *Hawaii* and *Hawaii Receipts* as well as a *Hawaii Agenda* Word document along with several photos. The search will also highlight your search word in the results.

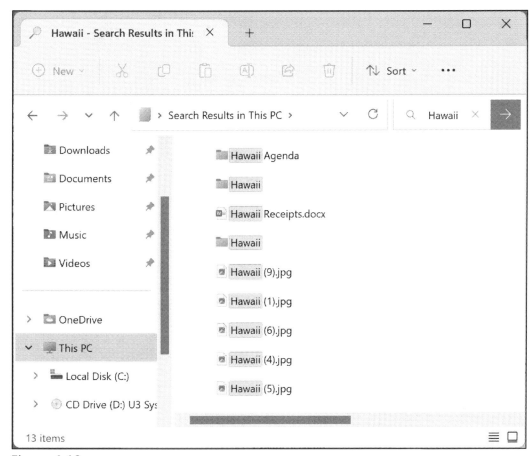

Figure 4.12

If you are not finding what you are looking for regarding your search results, keep in mind that there are much more advanced ways to search for files and folders such as by date or file type etc. So if you are feeling brave, you can research how to do these more advanced searches.

Changing Display Views

When looking at your files and folders in File Explorer, you might find that they are not being displayed in a way that is easy to see which might make them harder to work with.

Fortunately, you can change the way your files and folders are displayed, making them easier to see. From the icons\menus at the top of the File Explorer window, you can click on the *View* button to change how they are displayed.

Figure 4.13 shows the Large icons view which works well for pictures so you can see a preview of them before opening one. That way you don't need to go through all of them one at a time to find what you are looking for.

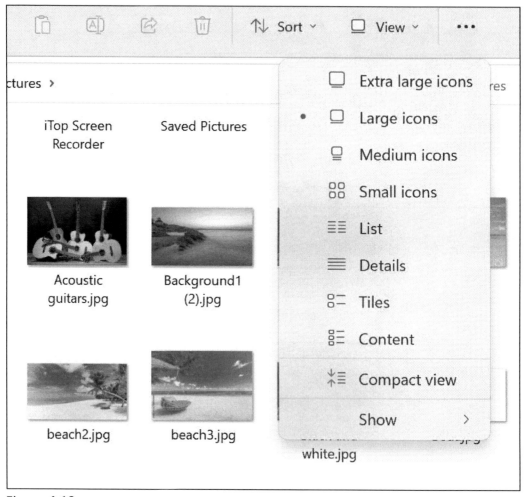

Figure 4.13

Figure 4.14 shows the *Details* view which will show you details such as the date the file was created, the type of file it is and its size etc.

Name	Date	Type	Size
Biking	11/16/2022 8:35 AM	File folder	
Camera Roll	11/16/2022 8:57 AM	File folder	
Dogs	11/16/2022 8:35 AM	File folder	
Hawaii	11/16/2022 8:35 AM	File folder	
iTop Screen Recorder	12/13/2022 9:38 AM	File folder	
Saved Pictures	11/16/2022 8:57 AM	File folder	
Screenshots	11/16/2022 8:35 AM	File folder	
Trails	11/16/2022 8:35 AM	File folder	
Acoustic guitars.jpg	6/10/2022 8:15 AM	JPG File	130 KB
Background1 (2).jpg	4/17/2015 12:20 PM	JPG File	1,417 KB

Figure 4.14

You can have different views configured for different folders and the settings should stay in place when you close the folder and then go back into it. I would play with the different view settings to find the ones that work the best for you.

Copying and Moving Files and Folders
While working with your files you will most likely come across a situation where a file or folder is in the wrong place and needs to be moved or you would like to make a copy of a document to edit so you can keep the original as is with its current information.

Copying and moving files or folders is a fairly simple process and once you do it a few times, it should become pretty easy to get the hang of. There are several ways to do this, but I will just go over the two most common.

First, you will need to decide if you are going to copy a file (or folder) or if you are going to move it. Copying it will make an exact duplicate in another location or folder while moving it will move it to a new location and remove it from its previous location.

To copy a file or folder, all you need to do is right click on it and then click on the copy icon as seen in figure 4.15. You won't see anything happen to the file, so you just need to assume that it has been copied.

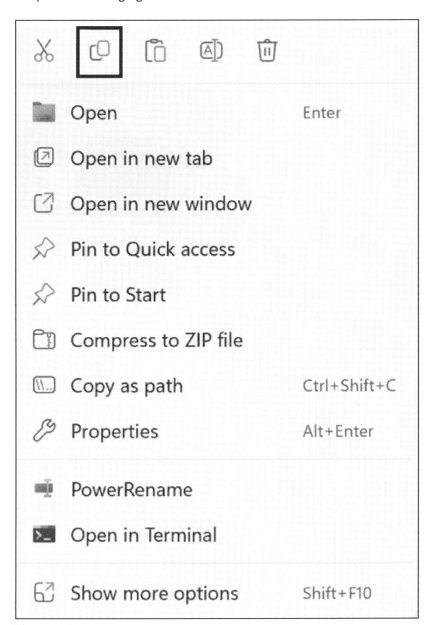

Figure 4.15

Then go to the location where you want to copy the file or folder to and right click in any blank area and choose the Paste icon.

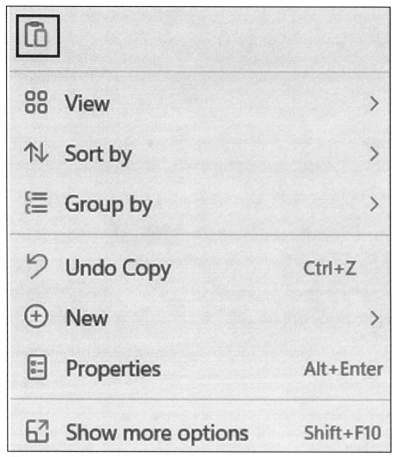

Figure 4.16

If you want to move the file or folder rather than copy it, you will choose the Cut option (scissors icon) rather than Copy. When you cut a file or folder, you will notice that its icon changes to a faded version. This indicates that it has been cut and is ready to move elsewhere. Then you would paste it the same way as if you were copying it.

Figure 4.17

If you change your mind after clicking copy or cut, you don't need to do anything to cancel the process as long as you don't choose the paste option. You can also press the Esc key on your keyboard to cancel the process.

If you want to try a faster way to copy or move a file or folder, then you can try the keyboard shortcuts rather than the right click method. Keyboard shortcuts are used to accomplish the same tasks you would do with your mouse, except everything is done on the keyboard instead.

To do so, simply select the file or folder and then press **Ctrl-C** on your keyboard to copy or **Ctrl-X** to cut. Then when you get to your destination you can press **Ctrl-V** to paste.

Chapter 5 - Microsoft Edge Web Browser

A big part of using a computer for many people is being able to go online to do things such as check email, go shopping, communicate with friends and family and so on. In fact, I would say that using the internet is the most common thing that anyone does on their computer!

In order to access the internet, you will need to use software called a web browser. This software allows you to go to whatever website you wish to access and perform searches as well.

One thing that many people tend to get mixed up is web browsers and search engines. These are two different things so it's important to understand how they differ.

A web browser is the software used to access the internet while a search engine is the website used within a web browser to perform online searches. So you will open your web browser and then go to the website of the search engine.

There are various web browsers such as Microsoft Edge, Google Chrome and Firefox etc. There are also many search engines such as Bing, Google and Yahoo etc. As I go along in this chapter, things should begin to make more sense.

Microsoft Edge is the web browser that comes preinstalled with windows. Since this chapter is about the Edge web browser, that is what I will be using for my examples. This doesn't mean you are stuck using Edge for your web browser if you are used to using a different one. And if you want to use more than one web browser on your computer, that is possible as well.

The Edge Interface

In order to get the most out of the Edge web browser, you should know how to find the various areas that make up the browser itself. Figure 5.1 shows the Edge browser with the Bing search engine page open. For now we are not going to worry about everything that is going on with this page but rather the key components of the browser itself which can all be found at the top of the browser (figure 5.2).

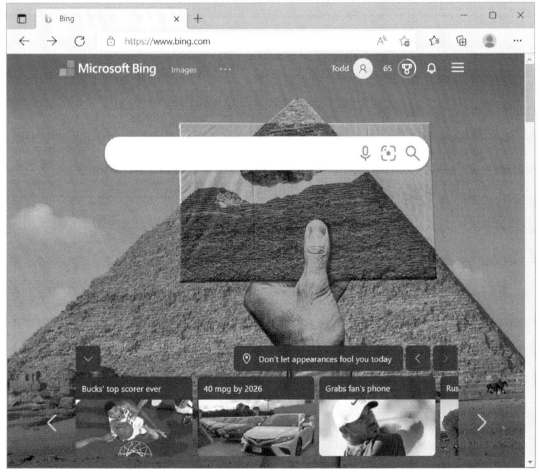

Figure 5.1

Figure 5.2

Figures 5.3 and 5.4 show both ends of the top of the Edge browser enlarged to make it easier to see. They are also marked up with the components that make up the browser.

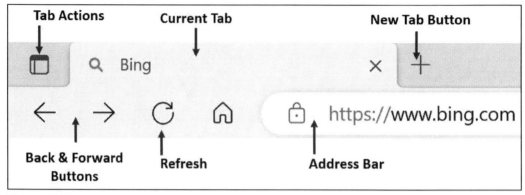

Figure 5.3

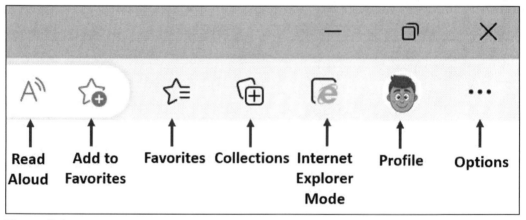

Figure 5.4

Here is an explanation of what each of these sections does. Keep in mind that there will most likely be a few that you will never use and that Microsoft frequently changes what icons are shown so yours might be missing some or have some extras that are not shown.

- **Tab Actions** – Here you can do things such as search your open tabs or reopen tabs that you recently closed.

- **Current Tab** – This is the tab that you are currently looking at. All modern web browsers will let you open multiple tabs so you can have a different website open in each one and then just switch in between them as needed. Figure 5.5 shows the Edge browser with four different tabs open at the same time.

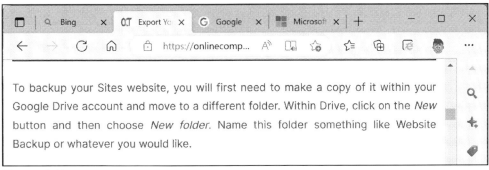

Figure 5.5

- **New Tab Button** – Clicking on the **+** next to a tab will open a new tab that you can then use to go to a different website without having to leave the current site you are on within your other open tab(s).

- **Back & Forward Buttons** – As you click around on a website to go to other pages or sections, you can use the back and forward buttons to navigate to previous pages that you were on.

- **Refresh** – Many websites will contain information that constantly changes, such as news sites. You can use the refresh button to update the current page you are on. You can also use the F5 key on your keyboard to do the same thing.

- **Address Bar** – This will display the website address of the site you are currently viewing. You can also type in a different website address such as **google.com** and press enter on your keyboard to take you to that site. Just be sure to spell it right or you might end up somewhere you don't want to go!

- **Read Aloud** – You can have the current webpage you are on read out loud to you by Edge if you would rather not read it yourself.

- **Add to Favorites** – If you want to keep this page in your browser so you can easily access it later, then you can add it to your favorites. Edge uses the term favorites while other web browsers use the term bookmarks. Regardless of the term, they both mean the same thing.

- **Favorites** – Here you can view and open any websites that you have saved in your browser.

- **Collections** – Collections are a way to save web pages and then also add things like notes and pictures at the same time.

- **Internet Explorer Mode** – This can be used to open websites using the older Internet Explorer interface for backwards compatibility.

- **Profile** – Here you can find and manage information about your Microsoft account if you are signed in. You don't need to be signed in to use Edge.

- **Options** – There are many upon many options that you can use to configure how Edge works, but you most likely will never need to change any of them.

You might have noticed that there is no Home button in Edge which is used to take you back to your home page from any website with a click of the button. You can enable the Home button from the Edge settings under the *start, home and new tabs* section.

Using Tabs

Tabbed browsing is the process of opening different websites within individual tabs that you can then switch back and forth between as needed.

Many people like to view multiple websites while browsing the internet and if we had to use the back and forward buttons to navigate these various sites each time we wanted to refer to a different site, that would make things really difficult. Back before browser tabs, we had to open multiple copies of our browser in order to have multiple websites open at the same time.

Let's say you were shopping on Amazon for a blender and wanted to compare the price of that blender at Target. Rather than view it on Amazon and then close the page to see it on the Target website, you can simply open a new tab and have both of them open at the same time.

Figure 5.6 shows the Amazon page open with the blender I am looking for. You can see at the top of the image that there is only one tab open and it's set to the Amazon website.

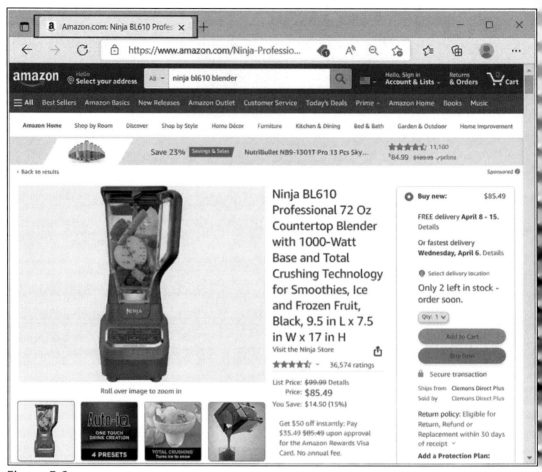

Figure 5.6

If I were to click on the + next to that open tab, I would then get a new page where I can either perform a search or type in a website address in the address bar such as **target.com**. Once I get to the Target website, I can search for the same blender and see the price and other details so I can compare it with Amazon (figure 5.7).

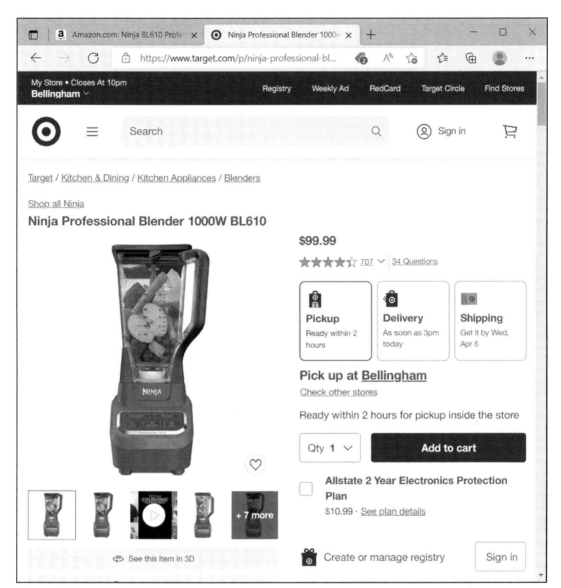

Figure 5.7

Now I can click on either tab to switch back and forth between the Amazon blender page and the Target blender page. If I want to close a tab, all I need to do is click on the X at the right side of the tab.

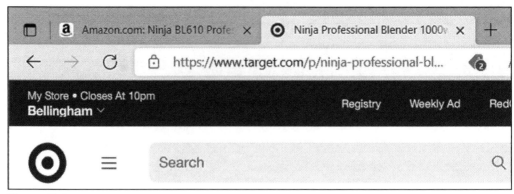

Figure 5.8

Adding and Using Favorites

There are millions of websites out there on the world wide web and it's hard enough remembering the few that you go to on a daily basis! Fortunately, we can keep track of our frequently visited websites by adding them to our favorites. Favorites are also known as bookmarks in other web browsers such as Google Chrome but both terms mean the exact same thing.

In order to save a website to your favorites, you will first need to go to that website within your browser. I will go to **onlinecomputertips.com** in my browser and once I am there, I will click on the add to favorites button. As you can see in figure 5.9, if you hover your mouse over any of the buttons, it will tell you what it is used for.

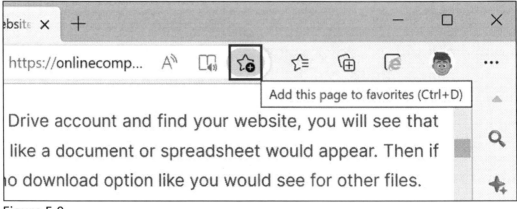

Figure 5.9

When I click on the add to favorites button, I will be given the opportunity to either keep the name of the favorite that Edge takes from the website or type in my own name. I can also add the favorite to the default Favorites bar or add it to another subfolder if I happen to have any.

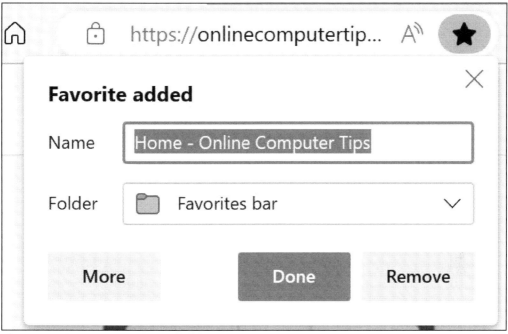

Figure 5.10

After I click on the *Done* button, the website will be added to my favorites and when I click on the *show favorites* button, it will be displayed with any other favorites I might have. Figure 5.11 shows that this I have this new website as well as the Microsoft website as my only favorites.

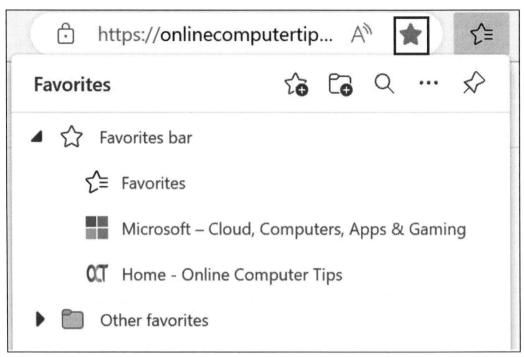

Figure 5.11

You will also notice that the star icon will change to a solid blue the next time you go to the page indicating that this webpage is already in your favorites.

Figure 5.12

Since I chose to add my new favorite to the Favorite Bar as seen in figure 5.10, it will now be shown within Edge itself under the address bar and I can simply click on it to be taken directly to that website.

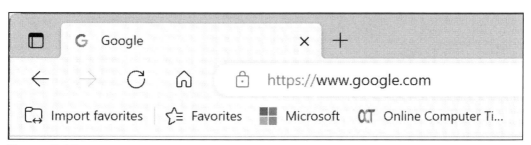

Figure 5.13

Searching and Search Results
One of the main things people do with a web browser is perform searches. If you don't know the particular website that you want to go to then you will most likely need to search for sites that contain the information you need.

When you open your web browser, it will take you to your home page which will most likely be the Edge home page or the Bing website since Bing is Microsoft's own search engine. Either way, you will have a search box on the page for any search engine you use.

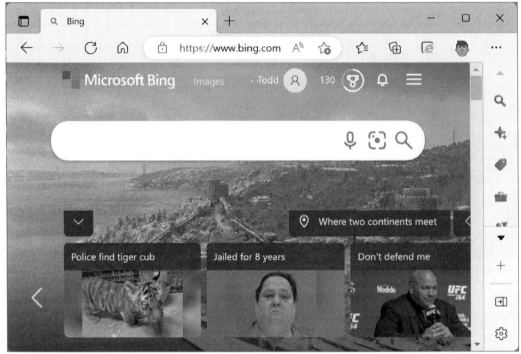

Figure 5.14

Then you can type in your search term and press the Enter key on your keyboard to be taken to the results. If I were to type Australian Shepherd for my search term and press enter, I would get results similar to figure 5.16.

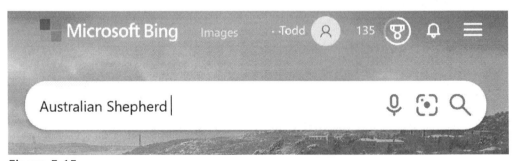

Figure 5.15

Since the default search engine for Edge is Bing, I get the results that they provide including some pictures, information and videos.

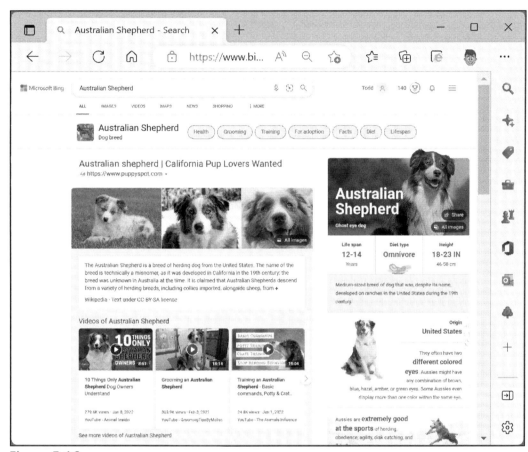

Figure 5.16

If I scroll down the page, I will then see the search results that I can click on to take me to websites that have information on Australian Shepherds.

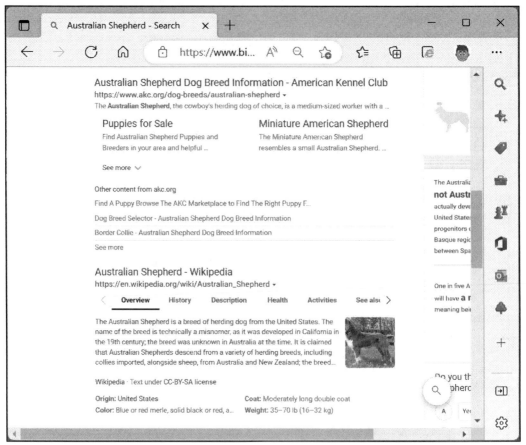

Figure 5.17

If I were to perform the same search using the Google search engine, I would get different results as shown in figure 5.18.

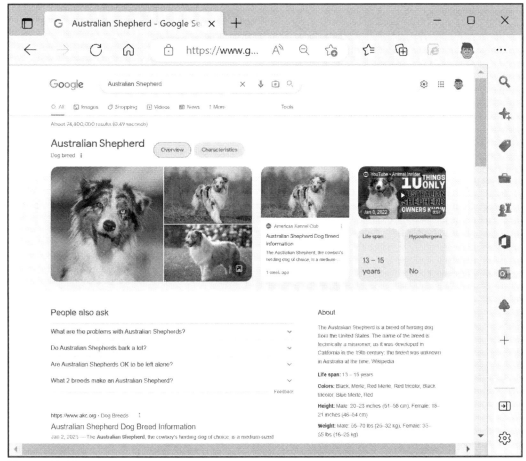

Figure 5.18

Saving Pictures from Websites

While visiting certain websites, you might find pictures that are of interest to you and that you would like to save on your computer so you can view them later or even email them to friends and family.

Saving (downloading) a picture from a webpage is a fairly easy thing to do and it only takes a couple of steps to complete the process. The first thing you need to do is find the picture you want to save on a webpage. Next, you will right click on the picture and then choose the *Save image as* option.

Figure 5.19

Then you will need to navigate to the folder on your computer where you want to save the picture to. Where it says *File name*, you can stick with the actual name of the file from the website, or you can change the name to something you prefer by erasing the given name and typing in your own.

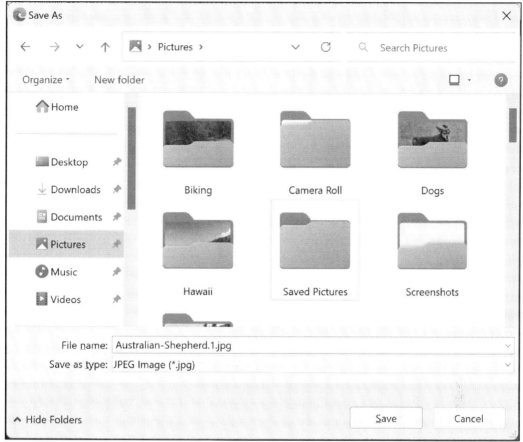

Figure 5.20

After you save the picture, you can go to that folder and open it from there or attach it to an email etc.

If you find that you are unable to save a picture from a website or that there is no *Save image as* option, that could mean that the website owner has made it so people cannot download pictures from their website, usually for legal or copyright reasons.

Sharing Websites With Others

If you are the type who likes to spend a lot of time "surfing" the internet, you will most likely come across a situation where you find a website that you would like to share with a friend, or you maybe even found an item online that would like to suggest someone buy you for your upcoming birthday!

There are a couple of ways to share a website but most likely you will be doing it via email since that is the most common. Once you are on the website you wish to share, you will need to copy the address of the website so you can then paste it into an email and then send it off to whoever you want to share it with.

To copy an address you can click inside the address bar at the top of the window, so the text is highlighted blue.

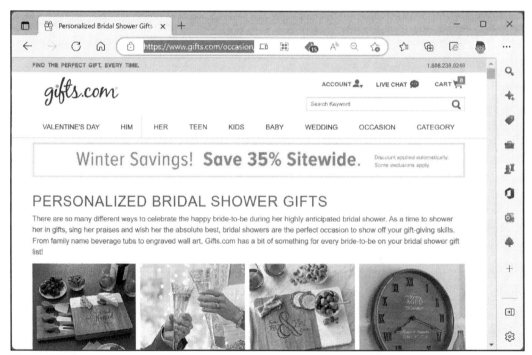

Figure 5.21

Then you can right click on the highlighted text and choose the *Copy* option.

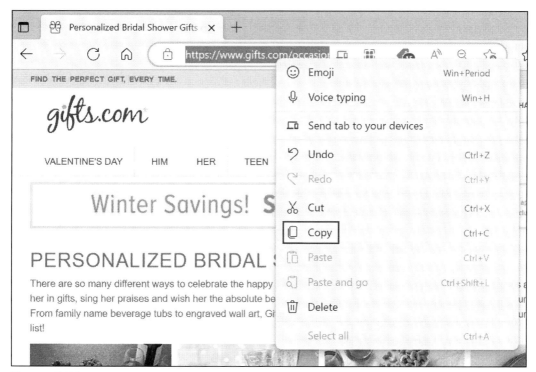

Figure 5.22

From here, you would open a new email and right click within the email body and choose the *Paste* option. Figure 5.23 shows how it would look in a Gmail email, but yours will look a little different if you are not using Gmail.

If you are interested in learning how to get the most out of your Gmail account, then check out my book titled **Gmail Made Easy**.
https://www.amazon.com/dp/B09PW3TRMX

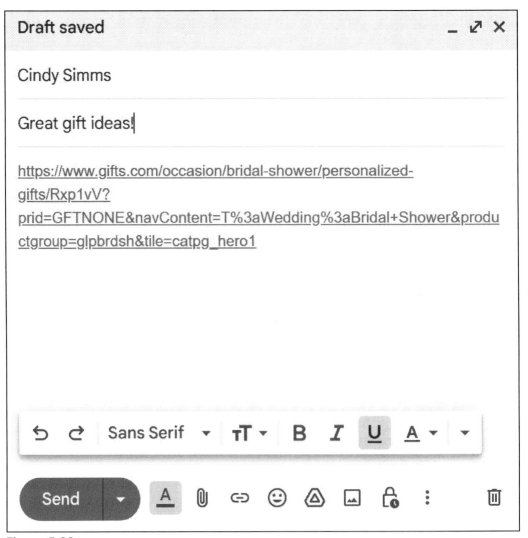

Figure 5.23

Another way to share a website in Edge is to click on the ellipsis (...) at the upper right hand corner of the page and then choose the *Share* option.

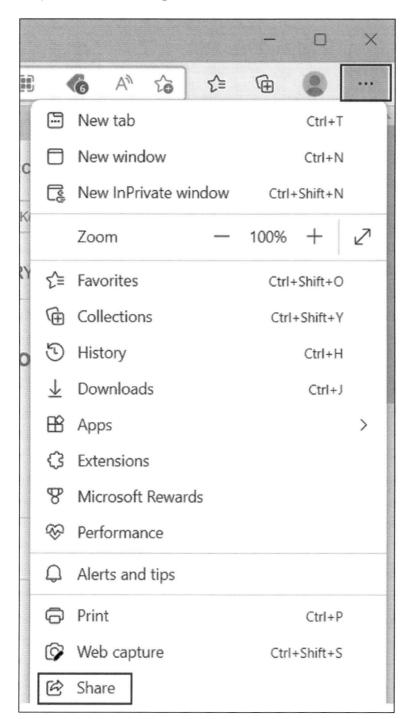

Figure 5.24

From here you will be given many options as to how you want to share the page. Keep in mind that some of these options might not apply to you. For example, if you don't have a Twitter account, you will not be able to share a website that way. At the top of the list, you will have a *Copy link* option that will do the same thing as you saw in the previous sharing method.

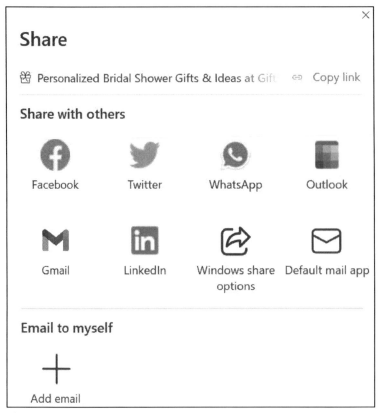

Figure 5.25

Chapter 6 – Extras

There is a lot more to Microsoft Windows 11 than I have discussed in this book so far but in order to make it so it's not overly complicated I of course had to leave out a lot of the more technical information.

However, there are still some additional topics I wanted to discuss that don't really fit into any of the other chapters, so I decided to give these topics their own chapter.

If you feel like taking your Windows 11 skills to the next level, then check out my book titled **Windows 11 Made Easy**.
https://www.amazon.com/dp/B09HFXWXRY

Printing

Most computer owners have a printer connected to their PC so they can print out things such as documents, emails or articles they found online. Some people even have more than one printer which allows them greater control over how their print jobs work based on the type of printer they print to.

There are two main types of printers that the average home user will use for their print jobs, and these are inkjet printers and laser printers.

Inkjet printers use replaceable and sometimes refillable ink cartridges, and the black ink will be its own cartridge and the colors all be in one cartridge as well or separated into yellow, cyan and magenta. The printers themselves are fairly cheap and often you will find that replacing the ink costs almost as much as the printer itself!

You can get an inkjet printer that is just meant for printing (figure 6.1), or you can get what is called an all-in-one printer that will also copy, scan and fax as seen in figure 6.2.

Figure 6.1

Figure 6.2

Inkjet printers work fine for most people and the quality is usually pretty good.

Laser printers offer higher quality print jobs at a higher price for the printer itself. They use a different technology to print which results in a crisper, higher resolution print job. A black and white laser printer can cost more than a color inkjet printer. And a color laser printer can easily cost several hundred dollars. Plus the toner cartridges can be very expensive as well.

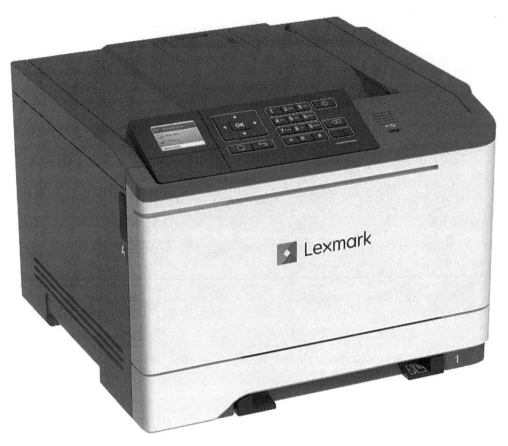

Figure 6.3

The process for printing a document, photo, email etc. is pretty much the same but there will be some differences depending on what you are printing from. The biggest challenge will be finding where the print option is.

Figure 6.4 shows how you print a webpage in Microsoft Edge, figure 6.5 shows how to print an email from Gmail and figure 6.6 shows how to print from Microsoft Word.

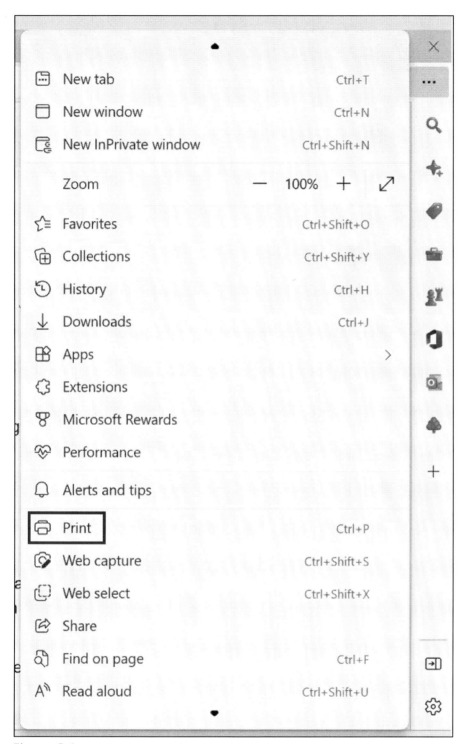

Figure 6.4

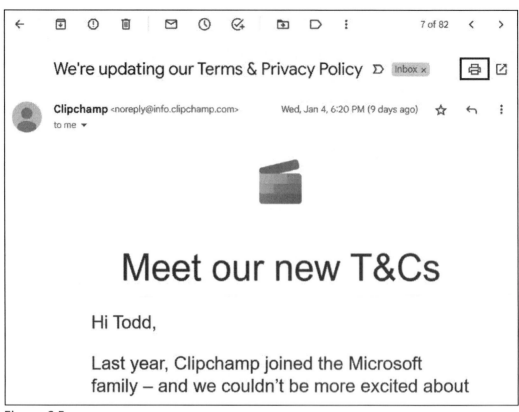

Figure 6.5

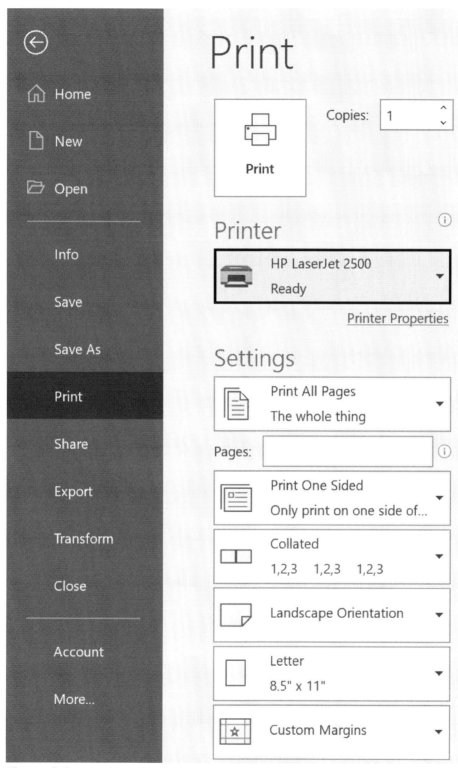

Figure 6.6

If you are having trouble finding the print option, you can press Ctrl-P on your keyboard to bring up the print settings for most programs. If you have more than one printer, you can then click on the dropdown arrow and choose which printer you would like to use for the particular print job.

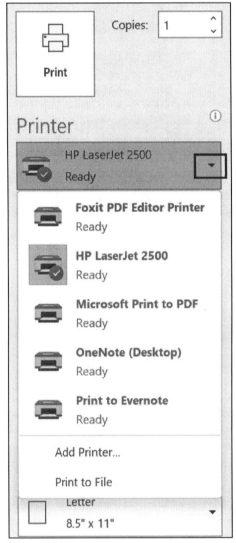

Figure 6.7

If you look at figure 6.7, you will see an option for *Microsoft Print to PDF*. This can be used from any program to create a PDF file from whatever document or page you are trying to print.

Changing Your Computer's Date or Time

The date and time on your computer are used for many things such as tracking when you updated a document or received an email. So if either of these is incorrect, you will not have accurate information on your computer.

Generally, your computer should keep accurate time and Windows will actually go out to the internet and use trusted time servers (computers) to make sure that it is using the correct date and time.

However, you might come across a situation where your date or time is not correct. Or if you take your computer to another location in a different time zone, things might not update automatically.

If you need to change the date or time, it's very easy to do and only takes a few clicks to do so.

If you right click on the clock at the lower right hand corner of the screen, you should have an option that says Adjust date and time that you can click on to bring up the settings as shown in figure 6.9.

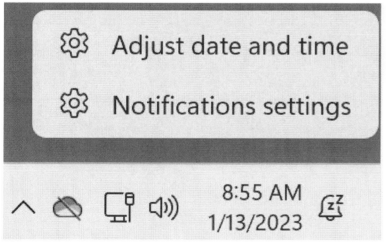

Figure 6.8

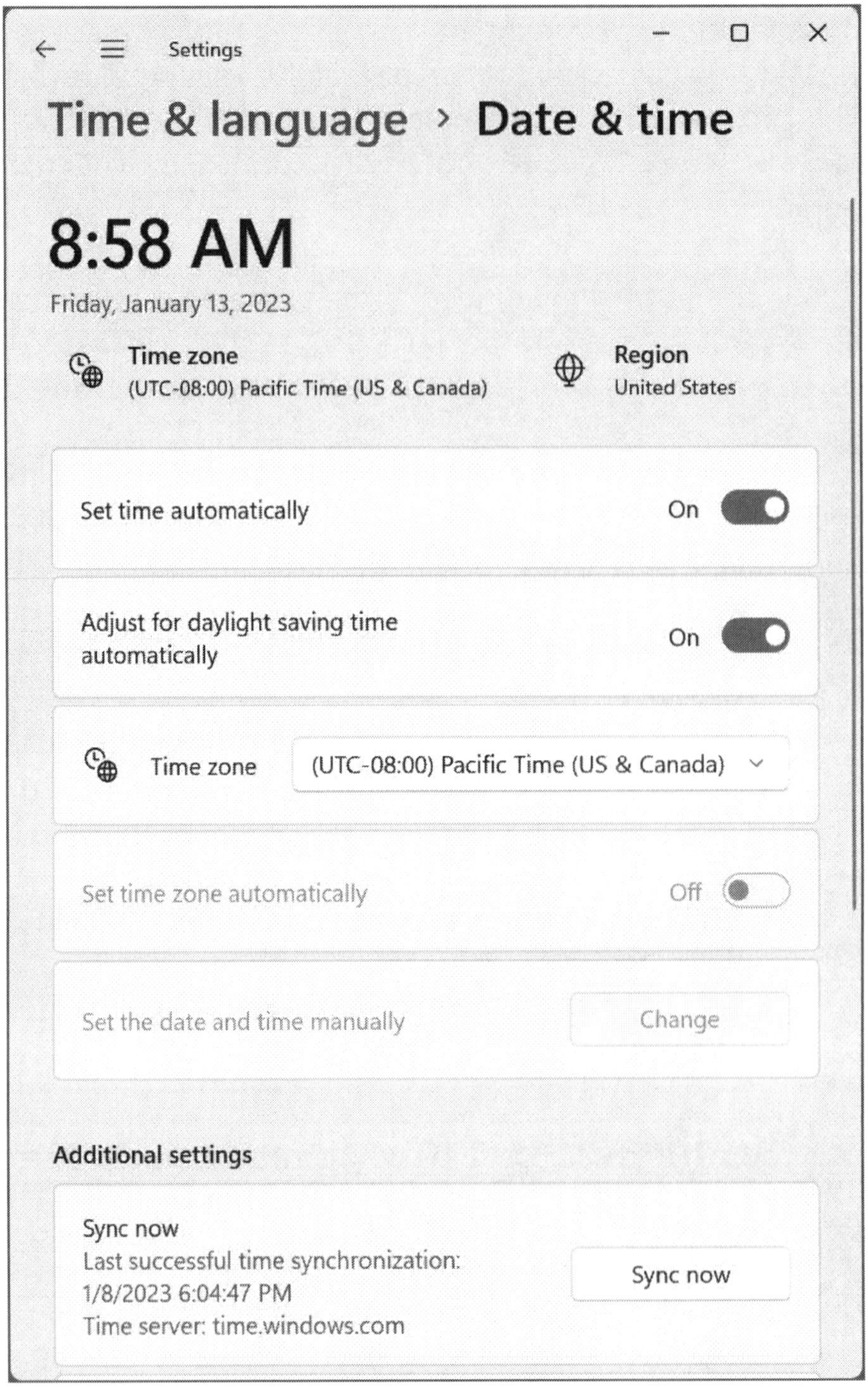

← ≡ Settings   − □ ✕

Time & language › Date & time

8:58 AM
Friday, January 13, 2023

🌐 **Time zone**
(UTC-08:00) Pacific Time (US & Canada)

🌐 **Region**
United States

Set time automatically	On ⬤

Adjust for daylight saving time automatically	On ⬤

🌐   Time zone   (UTC-08:00) Pacific Time (US & Canada) ⌄

Set time zone automatically	Off ◯

Set the date and time manually	Change

Additional settings

Sync now
Last successful time synchronization:
1/8/2023 6:04:47 PM
Time server: time.windows.com

Sync now

Figure 6.9

From here you can do things such as have Windows set your computer's time automatically and adjust for daylight savings automatically which should be enabled by default. You can also change your time zone if it's wrong because that will make your time show incorrectly on your computer.

If you disable the *Set time automatically* option, then you will be able to click on the *Change* button in the *Set the date and time manually* section. Then you will be able to set the date and time yourself as shown in figure 6.10.

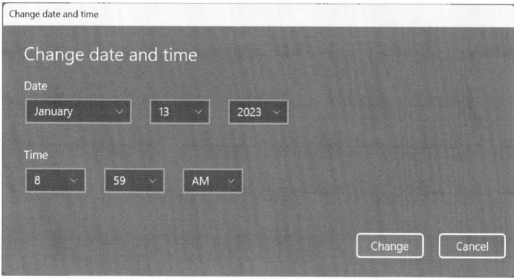

Figure 6.10

The Recycle Bin

Throwing away trash is just a way of life, and this also applies to files and folders on your computer that you no longer need. If we were forced to keep every picture or document we ever downloaded then we would run out of space rather quickly on our computers.

Fortunately, you can delete any file or folder you like if you feel it's not necessary to keep. Now, this doesn't mean you can simply go into File Explorer and start deleting things randomly to free up space on your hard drive. If you delete the wrong file or folder, you can make your computer inoperable.

If you do delete a file or folder and then realize that you didn't mean to or change your mind, you can go back into your "trash" and restore it if needed. This trash can is called the Recycle Bin and you have most likely seen the icon on your desktop.

Figure 6.11

If you double click on the Recycle Bin, you will be shown any files or folders that you have deleted. You can sort this list by name or date deleted etc. as needed to help you find what you are looking for. To do this, simply click on the column header (name) to sort by that attribute. If you click on Name, it will sort alphabetically from A to Z and if you click it again, it will sort from Z to A. You can also see where the file or folder was deleted from in the *Original location* column.

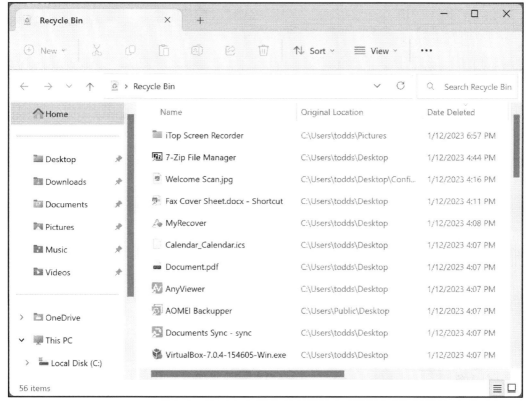

Figure 6.12

To restore an item, you can either right click on it and choose *Restore* or click on it once to highlight it and choose the *Restore the selected items* option at the top of the window. The *Restore all items* option will restore all of the contents of the Recycle Bin to their original locations but you will most likely never use this option.

Figure 6.13

Like I just mentioned, when you restore a file or folder, it will be put back in its original location so make sure you look in the *Original Location* column before restoring it, so you know where to find it. You can also drag an item out of the Recycle Bin to the desktop or another folder if you want to have it restored to a different location.

If you realize that you don't need to keep any of the files or folders in the Recycle Bin, you can click on the *Empty Recycle Bin* button at the top of the window to have everything removed. Just keep in mind that if you realize you needed something back, you will not be able to recover it without special software and even that is not guaranteed.

Connecting your Smartphone to Your Computer
Most people who use a smartphone use it for their camera rather than having a separate digital camera for photos. If you want to transfer pictures and videos from your phone to your computer, it's a pretty easy process to do. Just keep in mind that you can either COPY pictures from your phone to your computer, or you can MOVE them. Copying them won't free up any space from your phone but moving them will.

The first step in the process is to connect the USB cable that came with your phone to the normal charging port on your phone, and then to a free USB port on your computer.

Figure 6.14

The next step involves telling your phone that you want to use the connection to your computer to transfer files. This is usually done by pulling down from the notification area, tapping on the USB section (figure 6.15) to open up the connection options, and choosing the appropriate action (figure 6.16). In my example, I am using an Android smartphone so the screenshots and the process will look a little different for iPhones.

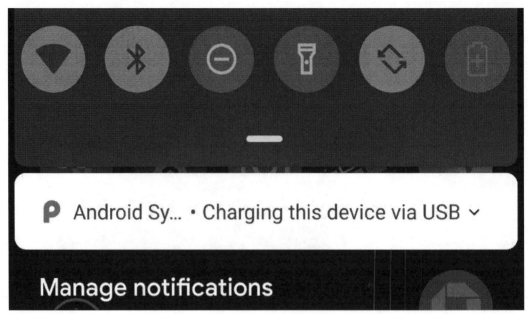

Figure 6.15

Notice in figure 6.16 that I chose the *File Transfer* option because I want to transfer files from my phone to my computer. You may see options with slightly different names such as photo transfer, for example.

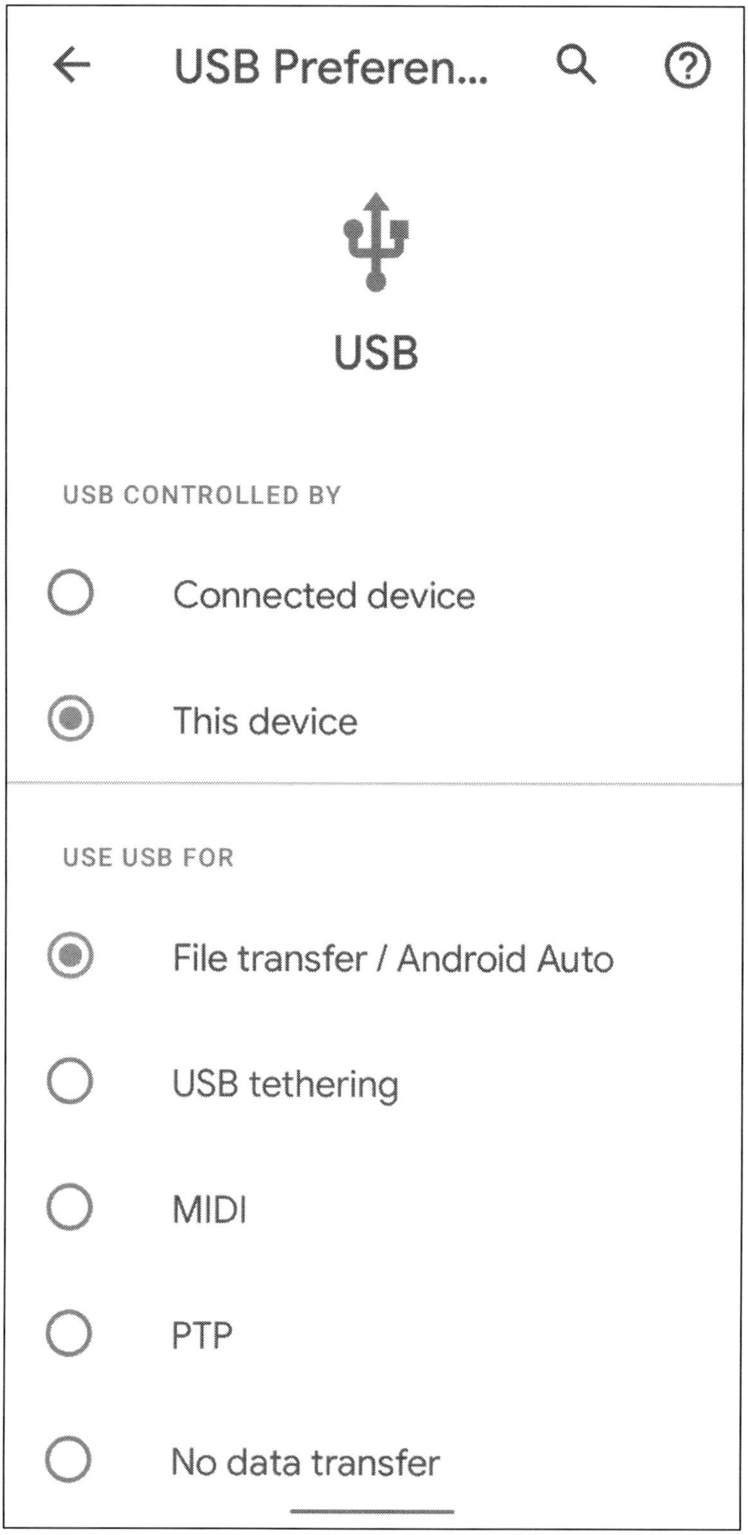

←   USB Preferen...   🔍   ⦵

USB

USB CONTROLLED BY

○   Connected device

◉   This device

USE USB FOR

◉   File transfer / Android Auto

○   USB tethering

○   MIDI

○   PTP

○   No data transfer

Figure 6.16

Then on my computer, I should see my phone appear. Then I can double click on its internal storage to see the files and folders contained on my phone.

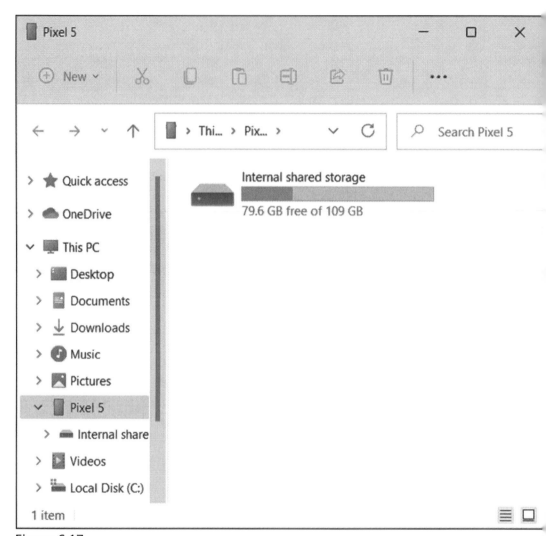

Figure 6.17

The folder I want to look for is named DCIM, and when I find that, I want to double click it to open it up.

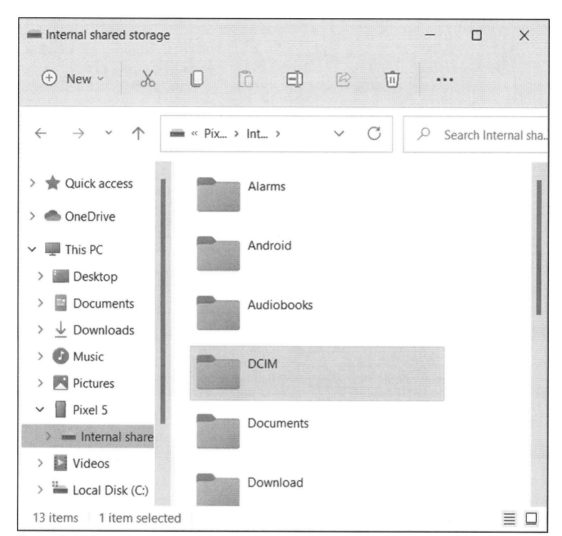

Figure 6.18

Within that folder you may see your pictures, or you might have another folder called Camera that you will need to open up. Once you are here, you can drag and drop the pictures from your phone to your computer and then delete them off of your phone after you confirm that they have been copied over. You can delete them using the phone, or you can delete them right from this DCIM folder that you opened up on your computer.

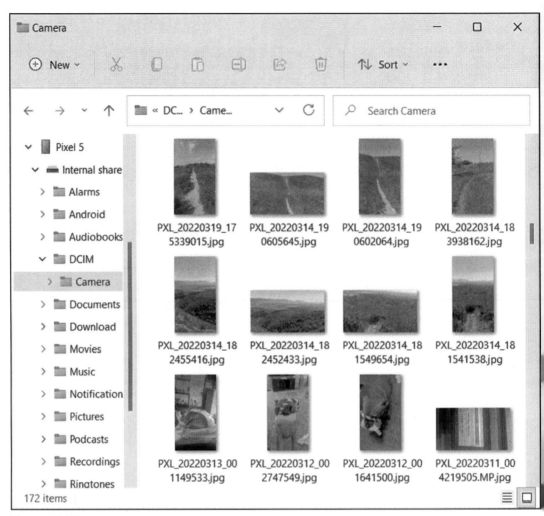

Figure 6.19

If you are looking for pictures that were sent via text message or saved from taking screenshots, then you can look for a folder named *Pictures* rather than DCIM and inside that folder you should find what you are looking for.

Signing Out and Locking Your Computer

Most home users will either just leave their computer on all day or shut it down when they are finished. If you use your computer off and on all day long, you might as well leave it on since they don't use too much power. And if you have your monitor set to power off after a certain interval of non-usage, that's even better.

But what if you have multiple people using your computer and they each have their own login? Or what if you don't want the kids or grandkids touching your computer when you are away? This is where logging off and locking your computer comes into play.

Logging off is the process of closing all the programs you have open and then signing you off your computer but leaving the computer on. This can be used if you want to let someone else log into the computer with their account and not have any of your programs or files left open.

Locking the computer will allow you to leave everything you are working on open but lock the screen so nobody can get into your computer without entering your password. Then when you unlock the computer with your usual password, everything is right where you left it.

Both of these options can be found by clicking on the Start button, then your username, and selecting the action you want to take as seen in figure 6.20. In my example, I have other users on this computer so that is why there are multiple names. If you are the only person configured on your computer, you will not see any additional usernames.

Figure 6.20

 It is possible for other people to log into the computer without you having to close everything you have open. To do this simply click on the Start button, your username and select their name from the list. They will then be logged in and all your work will stay open until you repeat this process using your username.

Connecting USB Devices to Your Computer

USB (Universal Serial Bus) is the most popular interface used for connecting devices to your computer. It is used for printers, flash drives, cameras, smartphones, keyboards, mice, gaming controllers and so on. All computers will have USB ports on the back, and most should have them on the front as well.

When it comes to connecting a device to a USB port, it doesn't matter which one you use. There are some faster USB ports called SuperSpeed and many times you will see an SS on the port indicating it's a faster port. These can be used with devices that support faster speeds, but you can still use them with any other devices.

Figure 6.21 shows a typical USB cable going into a USB port. This type of USB cable only goes one way, so you need to make sure it's right side up when plugging it in.

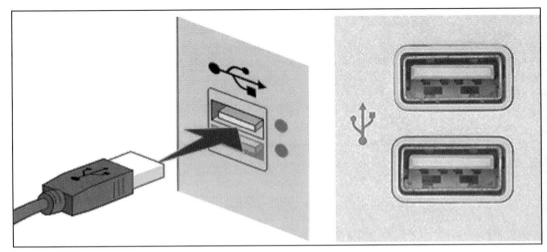

Figure 6.21

There are some other types of USB cables such as the type you connect to your printer as seen in figure 6.22 and the type you might use for your phone (figure 6.23).

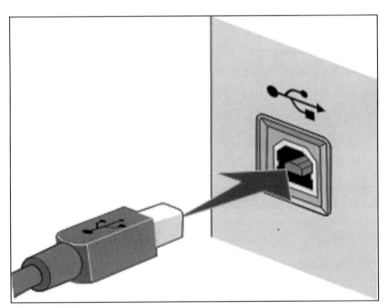

Figure 6.22

Figure 6.23

When you connect a new device to your computer, you might get a popup in the lower right hand corner of your screen saying Windows is configuring your new device and you might have to wait a moment for this process to complete.

For the most part, any USB device you connect to your computer should work without needing any extra intervention on your part. Some items such as printers will require that you install software, so Windows knows how to use your new printer. Other devices such as external hard drives or flash drives should open a new File Explorer window showing you the content of the drive so you can add or remove files to or from it.

Using WordPad to Type a Document
When typing documents on your computer, most people are familiar with the Microsoft Word software which is the most popular word processing software in use today. Word is part of the Microsoft Office Suite which also consists of Excel, PowerPoint, Outlook and so on. But

141

of course, if you wish to use any of this software, it will cost you a bit of money!

For those who need a basic word processor, they can use the built in WordPad app that comes with Windows. It has the basic functionality that is needed to type simple documents and add things such as pictures and charts etc. You can also perform basic formatting such as changing the font type, size and color and using bold, underline and italics.

One thing it does lack is a spelling and grammar checker so you will need to make sure you don't make any mistakes because WordPad will not let you know about them like Word will.

Figure 6.24 shows a basic WordPad document with some formatted text and an image added to the document. At the top of the page, you will find all of the formatting and insert options.

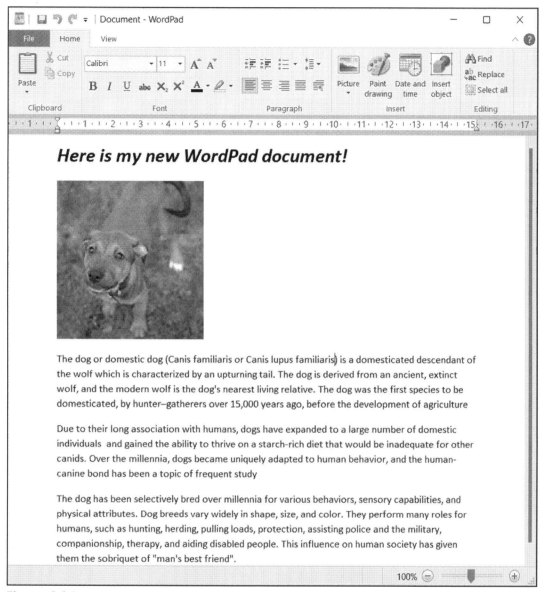

Figure 6.24

You can save your WordPad documents and they can be opened by other people using WordPad and can even be opened with the Word program itself.

Clicking on the *File* tab will give you some options for creating a new document, opening a recent document, saving, printing and page setup (figure 6.25).

Figure 6.25

Of course there are many other features that come with Windows 11, so don't be afraid to poke around the Start Menu and Settings to see what kind of treasures you can uncover!

What's Next?

Now that you have read through this book and taken your Windows 11 skills to the next level, you might be wondering what you should do next. Well, that depends on where you want to go. Are you happy with what you have learned, or do you want to further your knowledge or maybe get into some of the more advanced Windows 11 features?

If you do want to expand your knowledge on other computer-related topics, you should look at subject-specific books such as Microsoft Office, photo editing, Dropbox etc. Focus on one subject at a time, then apply what you have learned to the next subject. You can also check my other books that cover a wider range of topics mentioned above and then some.

There are many great video resources as well, such as Pluralsight or CBT Nuggets, which offer online subscriptions to training videos of every type imaginable. YouTube is also a great source for training videos if you know what to search for.

If you are content in being a Windows power user that knows more than your friends, then just keep on reading up on the technologies you want to learn, and you will soon become your friends and family's go-to computer person, which may or may not be something you want!

Thanks for reading Windows 11 Made Easy. You can also check out the other books in the Made Easy series for additional computer related information and training. You can get more information on my other books on my Computers Made Easy Book Series website.

https://www.madeeasybookseries.com

You should also check out my computer tips website, as well as follow it on Facebook to find more information on all kinds of computer topics.

www.onlinecomputertips.com
https://www.facebook.com/OnlineComputerTips/

About the Author

James Bernstein has been working with various companies in the IT for over 20 years, managing technologies such as SAN and NAS storage, VMware, backups, Windows Servers, Active Directory, DNS, DHCP, Networking, Microsoft Office, Exchange, and more.

He has obtained certifications from Microsoft, VMware, CompTIA, ShoreTel, and SNIA, and continues to strive to learn new technologies to further his knowledge on a variety of subjects.

He is also the founder of the website onlinecomputertips.com, which offers its readers valuable information on topics such as Windows, networking, hardware, software, and troubleshooting. Jim writes much of the content himself and adds new content on a regular basis. The site was started in 2005 and is still going strong today

Made in the USA
Columbia, SC
31 August 2023

22345231R00080